An authentic narrative of some remarkable and interesting particulars in the life of ********* communicated in a series of letters, to the Rev. Mr. Haweis, ... and by him (at the request of friends) now made public. The eighth edition.

John Newton

ECCO
PRINT EDITIONS

*An authentic narrative of some remarkable and interesting particulars in the life of *********
communicated in a series of letters, to the Rev. Mr. Haweis, ... and by him (at the request of
friends) now made public. The eighth edition.*
Newton, John
ESTCID: T105627
Reproduction from British Library
Anonymous. By John Newton, Rector of St. Mary, Woolnoth. The initial leaf contains an advertisement for books by John Newton.
London : printed for J. Johnson, 1792.
vii,[1],160p.,plates : map ; 12°

Eighteenth Century
Collections Online
Print Editions

Gale ECCO Print Editions

Relive history with *Eighteenth Century Collections Online*, now available in print for the independent historian and collector. This series includes the most significant English-language and foreign-language works printed in Great Britain during the eighteenth century, and is organized in seven different subject areas including literature and language; medicine, science, and technology; and religion and philosophy. The collection also includes thousands of important works from the Americas.

The eighteenth century has been called "The Age of Enlightenment." It was a period of rapid advance in print culture and publishing, in world exploration, and in the rapid growth of science and technology – all of which had a profound impact on the political and cultural landscape. At the end of the century the American Revolution, French Revolution and Industrial Revolution, perhaps three of the most significant events in modern history, set in motion developments that eventually dominated world political, economic, and social life.

In a groundbreaking effort, Gale initiated a revolution of its own: digitization of epic proportions to preserve these invaluable works in the largest online archive of its kind. Contributions from major world libraries constitute over 175,000 original printed works. Scanned images of the actual pages, rather than transcriptions, recreate the works *as they first appeared.*

Now for the first time, these high-quality digital scans of original works are available via print-on-demand, making them readily accessible to libraries, students, independent scholars, and readers of all ages.

For our initial release we have created seven robust collections to form one the world's most comprehensive catalogs of 18th century works.

Initial Gale ECCO Print Editions collections include:

History and Geography
Rich in titles on English life and social history, this collection spans the world as it was known to eighteenth-century historians and explorers. Titles include a wealth of travel accounts and diaries, histories of nations from throughout the world, and maps and charts of a world that was still being discovered. Students of the War of American Independence will find fascinating accounts from the British side of conflict.

Social Science

Delve into what it was like to live during the eighteenth century by reading the first-hand accounts of everyday people, including city dwellers and farmers, businessmen and bankers, artisans and merchants, artists and their patrons, politicians and their constituents. Original texts make the American, French, and Industrial revolutions vividly contemporary.

Medicine, Science and Technology

Medical theory and practice of the 1700s developed rapidly, as is evidenced by the extensive collection, which includes descriptions of diseases, their conditions, and treatments. Books on science and technology, agriculture, military technology, natural philosophy, even cookbooks, are all contained here.

Literature and Language

Western literary study flows out of eighteenth-century works by Alexander Pope, Daniel Defoe, Henry Fielding, Frances Burney, Denis Diderot, Johann Gottfried Herder, Johann Wolfgang von Goethe, and others. Experience the birth of the modern novel, or compare the development of language using dictionaries and grammar discourses.

Religion and Philosophy

The Age of Enlightenment profoundly enriched religious and philosophical understanding and continues to influence present-day thinking. Works collected here include masterpieces by David Hume, Immanuel Kant, and Jean-Jacques Rousseau, as well as religious sermons and moral debates on the issues of the day, such as the slave trade. The Age of Reason saw conflict between Protestantism and Catholicism transformed into one between faith and logic -- a debate that continues in the twenty-first century.

Law and Reference

This collection reveals the history of English common law and Empire law in a vastly changing world of British expansion. Dominating the legal field is the *Commentaries of the Law of England* by Sir William Blackstone, which first appeared in 1765. Reference works such as almanacs and catalogues continue to educate us by revealing the day-to-day workings of society.

Fine Arts

The eighteenth-century fascination with Greek and Roman antiquity followed the systematic excavation of the ruins at Pompeii and Herculaneum in southern Italy; and after 1750 a neoclassical style dominated all artistic fields. The titles here trace developments in mostly English-language works on painting, sculpture, architecture, music, theater, and other disciplines. Instructional works on musical instruments, catalogs of art objects, comic operas, and more are also included.

Lately published,

THE

POWER OF GRACE:

ILLUSTRATED IN SIX LETTERS,

From a Minister of the Reformed Church to
John Newton, Rector of St. *Mary, Woolnoth,* LONDON.
Translated from the original Latin, by *W. Cowper* of
the Inner Temple, Esq.

Printed for J. JOHNSON, in St. Paul's Church-
Yard. Price 2s. 6d. sewed.

Jos Collyer sculp

Gratia Prevalebit
Luke Ch. XIII v 7

AN

AUTHENTIC NARRATIVE

OF SOME REMARKABLE AND INTERESTING
PARTICULARS IN THE

LIFE OF ********

COMMUNICATED IN A SERIES OF

LETTERS,

TO THE REV. MR. HAWEIS, *Thomas*

RECTOR OF ALDWINCKLE, NORTHAMPTONSHIRE,

*And by him (at the Request of Friends) now
made public.*

I will bring the blind by a way that they knew not; I will
lead them in paths that they have not known; I will make
darkneſs light before them, and crooked things ſtrait.
Theſe things will I do unto them, and not forſake them.
Iſaiah xlii. 16.

I am as a wonder unto many. Pſalm lxxi. 7.

THE EIGHTH EDITION.

LONDON.
Printed for J. JOHNSON, Nº. 72, St. Paul's Church-Yard.

MDCCXCII.

PREFACE.

THE first of the following letters is so well adapted an introduction to the rest, that to trouble the reader with a long preface would be quite needless and impertinent. I will, therefore, detain him from entering upon the delightful and instructive relation which the following sheets present him with, little longer, than while I assure him that the narrative is quite genuine, and that the fol-

lowing

lowing letters were written to me at my requeſt. Some verbal relations of the facts awakened my curioſity to ſee a more connected account of them, which the author very obligingly conſented to, having, at that time, no intention of its being made public.—But the repeated ſolicitations of friends have at laſt prevailed; and, indeed, the publication is the more needful, as ſeveral imperfect copies have been handed about, and there has been cauſe to think ſome ſurreptitious edition might ſteal through the preſs into the hands of the public.

I have, therefore, with conſent of the author, now ſent theſe letters abroad in their original form. They were written in haſte as letters of friendſhip, to gratify my curioſity;
but

but the ſtyle, as well as the narrative itſelf, is ſo plain and eaſy, that
corrections were thought needleſs.
I can only add my beſt wiſhes, that
the great truths they contain may
prove as edifying, as the facts are
ſtriking and entertaining.

T. HAWEIS.

ALDWINCKLE, AUGUST, 1764.

LETTER I.

REVEREND AND DEAR SIR,

I MAKE no doubt but you have at times had pleafing reflections upon that promife made to the *Ifraelites*, Duet. viii. 2. They were then in the wildernefs, furrounded with difficulties, which were greatly aggravated by their own diftruft and perverfenefs: They had experienced a variety of difpenfations, the defign of which they could not as yet underftand, they frequently loft fight of God's gracious purpofes in their favour, and were much difcouraged by reafon of the way. To compofe and animate their minds, *Mofes* here fuggefts to them, that there was a fu-

A 5   ture

ture happy time drawing near, when their journey and warfare should be finished, that they should soon be put in possession of the promised land, and have rest from all their fears and troubles, and then it would give them pleasure to look back upon what they now found so uneasy to bear—" Thou shalt remember all the " way, by which the Lord thy God led " thee through this wilderness."

But the importance and comfort of these words is still greater, if we consider them in a spiritual sense, as addressed to all who are passing through the wilderness of this world to a heavenly *Canaan*; who by faith in the promises and power of God are seeking an eternal rest in that kingdom which cannot be shaken. The hope of that glorious inheritance inspires us with some degree of courage and zeal to press forward, to where Jesus has already entered as our forerunner, and when our eye is fixed upon him, we are more than conquerors over all that would withstand our progress. But we have not yet attained; we still feel the infirmities of a fallen nature: through the remains of ignorance and unbelief, we often mistake the Lord's dealings with

us,

us, and are ready to complain, when, if
we knew all, we fhould rather rejoice.
But to us likewife there is a time coming,
when our warfare fhall be accomplifhed,
our views enlarged, and our light increafed: then, with what tranfports of
adoration and love fhall we look back upon the way, by which the Lord led us!
We fhall then fee and acknowledge, that
mercy and goodnefs directed every ftep;
we fhall fee, that what our ignorance once
called adverfities and evils, were in reality
bleffings, which we could not have done
well without: that nothing befel us without a caufe: that no trouble came upon
us fooner, or preffed us more heavily, or
continued longer, than our cafe required:
in a word, that our many afflictions were
each in their place among the means employed by divine grace and wifdom, to
bring us to the poffeffion of that exceeding and eternal weight of glory, which
the Lord has prepared for his people.
And even in this imperfect ftate, though
we are feldom able to judge aright of
our prefent circumftances, yet, if we look
upon the years of our paft life, and compare the difpenfations we have been
brought through, with the frame of our

minds

minds under each fucceffive period; if we confider, how wonderfully one thing has been connected with another; fo that, what we now number amongft our great-eft advantages, perhaps, took their firft rife from incidents which we thought hardly worth our notice; and that we have fometimes efcaped the greateft dangers that threatened us, not by any wif-dom or forefight of our own, but by the intervention of circumftances, which we neither defired or thought of—I fay, when we compare and confider thefe things by the light afforded us in the Holy Scrip-ture, we may collect indifputable proof, from the narrow circle of our own concerns, that the wife and good providence of God watches over his people from the earlieft moment of their life, over-rules and guards them through all their wanderings in a ftate of ignorance, leads them in a way that they know not, till at length his providence and grace concur in thofe events and impreffions, which bring them to the knowledge of him, and themfelves.

I am perfuaded that every believer will, upon due reflection, fee enough in his own cafe to confirm this remark; but

not

not all in the fame degree. The outward
circumftances of many have been uniform, they have known but little variety
in life; and, with refpect to their inward
change, it has been effected in a fecret
way, unnoticed by others, and almoft un-
perceived by themfelves—The Lord has
fpoken to them, not in thunder and tem-
peft, but with a ftill fmall voice, he has
drawn them gradually to himfelf; fo that,
though they have a happy affurance of the
thing, that they know and love him, and
are paffed from death unto life; yet, of
the precife time and manner, they can
give little account. Others he feems to
felect, in order to fhew the exceeding riches
of his grace, and the greatnefs of his mighty
power: he fuffers the natural rebellion,
and wickednefs of their hearts to have full
fcope; while finners of lefs note are cut
off with little warning, thefe are fpared,
though finning with a high hand, and, as
it were, ftudying their own deftruction.
At length, when all that knew them are
perhaps expecting to hear, that they are
made fignal inftances of divine vengeance,
the Lord (whofe thoughts are high above
ours, as the heavens are higher than the
earth) is pleafed to pluck them as brands
out

out of the fire, and to make them monu-
ments of his mercy, for the encouragement of others: they are, beyond expectation, convinced, pardoned, and changed.
A case of this sort indicates a divine
power no less than the creation of a world:
it is evidently the Lord's doing, and it is
marvellous in the eyes of all those, who
are not blinded by prejudice and unbelief.

Such was the persecuting *Saul* · his
heart was full of enmity against *Jesus* of
Nazareth, and therefore he persecuted and
made havock of his disciples. He had
been a terror to the church of *Jerusalem*,
and was going to *Damascus* with the same
views — He was yet breathing out threatenings and slaughter against all that loved
the Lord *Jesus* — He thought little of the
mischief he had hitherto done — He was
engaged for the suppression of the whole
sect, and hurrying from house to house,
from place to place, he carried menaces
in his look, and repeated threatenings with
every breath. Such was his spirit and
temper, when the Lord *Jesus*, whom he
hated and opposed, checked him in the
height of his rage, called this bitter per-
secutor to the honour of an apostle, and
inspired him with great zeal and earnest-
ness,

nefs, to preach that faith, which he fo lately deftroyed.

Nor are we without remarkable difplays of the fame fovereign, efficacious grace in our own times—I may particularly mention the inftance of the late Colonel *Gardner*. If any real fatisfaction could be found in a finful courfe, he would have met with it; for he purfued the experiment with all poffible advantages—He was habituated to evil: and many uncommon, almoft miraculous deliverances, made no impreffion upon him. Yet *he* likewife was made willing in the day of God's power: and the bright example of his life, illuftrated and diffufed by the account of him, publifhed fince his death, has afforded an occafion of much praife to God, and much comfort to his people.

After the mention of fuch names, can you permit me, Sir, to add *my own?* If I do, it muft be with a very humbling diftinction. Thefe once eminent finners proved eminent Chriftians: much had been forgiven them, therefore they loved much. St. *Paul* could fay, " The grace beftowed " upon me was not in vain; for I la- " boured more abundantly than they all."

Colonel

Colonel *Gardner* likewife was as a city fet upon an hill, a burning and a fhining light: the manner of his converfion was hardly more fingular, than the whole courfe of his converfation from that time to his death. Here, alas, the parallel greatly fails! It has not been thus with me—I muft take deferved fhame to myfelf, that I have made very unfuitable returns for what I have received. But, if the queftion is only concerning the patience and long-fuffering of God, the wonderful interpofition of his providence in favour of an unworthy finner, the power of his grace in foftening the haideft heart, and the riches of his mercy in pardoning the moft enormous and aggravated tranfgreffions; in thefe refpects, I know no cafe more extraordinary than my own. And indeed more perfons, to whom I have related my ftory, have thought it worthy of being preferved.

I never gave any fuccinct account in writing, of the Lord's dealing with me, till very lately, for I was deterred, on the one hand, by the great difficulty of writing properly where *felf* is concerned; on the other, by the ill ufe which perfons of corrupt and perverfe minds are often known

to

to make of fuch inftances. The *Pfalmift*
reminds us that a referve in thefe things
is proper, when he fays, " Come unto me,
" all you *that fear God*, and I will tell you
" what he hath done for my foul," and
our Lord cautions us not to " caft our
pearls before fwine." The pearls of a
Chriftian are, perhaps, his choice experi-
ences of the Lord's power and love in the
concerns of his foul; and thefe fhould not
be at all adventures made public, left
we give occafion to earthly and groveling
fouls, to profane what they cannot underftand. Thefe were the chief reafons of my
backwardnefs; but a few weeks fince, I
yielded to the judgment and requeft of a
much refpected friend, and fent him a relation at large, in a feries of eight letters.
The event has been, what I little expected;
I wrote to one perfon, but my letters have
fallen into many hands: amongft others,
I find they have reached your notice; and
inftead of blaming me for being too tedious and circumftantial, which was the
fault I feared I had committed, you are
pleafed to defire a ftill more diftinct detail.
As you and others of my friends appre-
hend my compliance with this requeft
may be attended with fome good effect,
may

may promote the pleafing work of praife to our adorable Redeemer, or confirm the faith of fome or other of his people, I am willing to obey; I give up my own reafonings upon the inexpediency of fo inconfiderable a perfon as myfelf, adventuring in fo public a point of view. If God may be glorified on my behalf, and his children in any meafure comforted or inftructed, by what I have to declare of his goodnefs, I fhall be fatisfied; and am content to leave all other poffible confequences of this undertaking in his hands, who does all things well.

I muft again have recourfe to my memory, as I retained no copies of the letters you faw. So far as I can recollect what I then wrote, I will relate, but fhall not affect a needlefs variety of phrafe and manner, merely becaufe thofe have been already perufed by many. I may, perhaps in fome places, when repeating the fame facts, exprefs myfelf in nearly the fame words; yet I propofe according to your defire, to make this relation more explicit and particular than the former, efpecially towards the clofe, which I wound up haftily, left my friend fhould be wearied. I hope, you will likewife excufe me, if I do not
ftrictly

ftrictly confine myfelf to narration, but now and then interfperfe fuch reflections as may offer, while I am writing: and though you have fignified your intentions of communicating what I fend you to others, I muft not, on this account, affect a concifenefs and correctnefs, which is not my natural talent, left the whole fhould appear dry and conftrained. I fhall therefore (if poffible) think only of you, and write with that confidence and freedom which your friendfhip and candour deferve. This fheet may ftand as a preface, and I purpofe, as far as I can, to intermit many other engagements, until I have completed the tafk you have affigned me. In the mean time, I entreat the affiftance of your prayers, that in this, and all my poor attempts, I may have a fingle eye to his glory, who was pleafed to call me out of horrid darknefs into the marvellous light of his gofpel. I am, with fincere refpect,

Dear SIR,

Your obliged and affectionate fervant.

JANUARY 12, 1763.

LETTER

LETTER II.

I CAN fometimes feel a pleafure in repeating the grateful acknowledgment of
David, " O Lord, I am thy fervant, the
" fon of thine handmaid ; thou haft loofed
" my bands." The tender mercies, of
God, towards me, were manifeft in the
firft moment of my life—I was born as it
were in his houfe, and dedicated to him in
my infancy. My mother (as I have
heard from many) was a pious experienced
Chriftian, fhe was a diffenter, in communion with the late Dr. *Jennings.* I was her
only child, and as fhe was of a weak conftitution and a retired temper, almoft her
whole employment was the care of my
education. I have fome faint remembrance
of her care and inftructions. At a time
when I could not be more than three years
of age, fhe herfelf taught me *Englifh,* and
with fo much fuccefs, (as I had fomething
of a forward turn) that when I was four
years old, I could read with propriety in
any common book that offeied. She ftored
my

my memory, which was then very reten-
tive, with many valuable pieces, chapters,
and portions of fcripture, catechifms,
hymns, and poems. My temper, at that
time feemed quite fuitable to her wifhes:
I had little inclination to the noify fports
of children, but was beft pleafed when in
her company, and always as willing to
learn as fhe was to teach me. How far
the beft education may fall fhort of reach-
ing the heart, will ftrongly appear in the
fequel of my hiftory: yet, I think, for
the encouragement of pious parents to go
on in the good way, of doing their part
faithfully to form their children's minds,
I may properly propofe myfelf as an inftance. Though in procefs of time I finned away all the advantages of thefe
early impreffions, yet they were for a
great while a reftraint upon me; they
returned again and again, and it was very
long before I could wholly fhake them
off; and when the Lord at length opened
my eyes, I found a great benefit from
the recollection of them. Further, my
dear mother, befides the pains fhe took
with me, often commended me with
many prayers and tears to God; and I
doubt

doubt not but I reap the fruits of thefe prayers to this hour.

My mother obferved my early progrefs with peculiar pleafure, and intended from the fiift to bring me up with a view to the miniftry, if the Lord fhould fo incline my heart. In my fixth year I began to learn *Latin*; but, before I had time to know much about it, the intended plan of my education was broke fhort.—The Loid's defigns were far beyond the views of an earthly parent; he was pleafed to referve me for an unufual proof of his patience, providence, and grace, and theiefore over-ruled the purpofe of my friends, by depriving me of this excellent parent, when I was fomething under feven yeais old. I was boin the 24th of *July*, 1725, and fhe died the 11th of that month, 1732.

My father was then at fea, (he was a commander in the Mediterranean trade at that time:) he came home the following year, and foon after married again. Thus I paffed into different hands. I was well treated in all other refpects; but the lofs of my mother's inftructions was not repaired. I was now permitted to mingle with carelefs and profane children, and

foon

foon began to learn their ways. Soon after my father's marriage, I was fent to a boarding-fchool in *Effex*; where the imprudent feverity of the mafter almoft broke my fpirit and relifh for books. With him I forgot the firft principles and rules of arithmetic, which my mother had taught me years before. I ftaid there two years; in the laft of the two a new ufher coming, who obferved and fuited my temper, I took to the *Latin* with great eagernefs: fo that before I was ten years old, I reached and maintained the firft poft in the fecond clafs, which in that fchool read *Tully* and *Virgil*. I believe I was pufhed forward too faft, and therefore not being grounded, I foon loft all I had learnt (for I left fchool in my tenth year) and when I long afterwards undertook the *Latin* language from books, I think I had little, if any advantage, from what I had learnt before.

My father's fecond marriage was from a family in *Effex*; and when I was eleven years old, he took me with him to fea. He was a man of remarkable good fenfe, and great knowledge of the world; he took great care of my morals, but could not fupply my mother's part. Having been educated himfelf in *Spain*, he always obferved

ferved an air of diftance and feverity in his
carriage, which over-awed and difcouraged
my fpirit. I was always in fear when before him, and therefore he had the lefs influence. From that time to the year 1742,
I made feveral voyages, but with confiderable intervals between, which were
chiefly fpent in the country, excepting a
few months in my fifteenth year, when I
was placed upon a very advantageous profpect at *Alicant* in *Spain*; but my unfettled behaviour and impatience of reftraint
rendered that defign abortive.

In this period my temper and conduct
were exceedingly various. At fchool, or
foon after, I had little concern about religion, and eafily received very ill impreffions. But I was often difturbed with convictions, I was fond of reading from a
child, among other books, *Burnet's Chriftian Oratory* often came in my way; and
though I underftood but little of it, the
courfe of life therein recommended appeared very defirable, and I was inclined
to attempt it. I began to pray, to read
the fcripture, and to keep a fort of diary;
I was prefently religious in my own eyes;
but, alas! this feeming goodnefs had no
folid foundation, but paffed away like a
morning

morning cloud, or the early dew. I was
foon weary, gradually gave it up, and became worfe than before: inftead of prayer,
I learned to curfe and blafpheme, and was
exceedingly wicked, when from under my
parents' view. All this was before I was
twelve years old. About that time I had a
dangerous fall from a horfe; I was thrown
I believe, within a few inches of a hedge-
row newly cut down; I got no hurt, but
could not avoid taking notice of a gracious
providence in my deliverance; for had I
fell upon the ftakes, I had inevitably been
killed: my confcience fuggefted to me the
dreadful confequences, if in fuch a ftate
I had been fummoned to appear before
God. I prefently broke off from my profane practices, and appeared quite altered;
but it was not long before I declined
again. Thefe ftruggles between fin and
confcience were often repeated; but the
confequence was, that every relapfe funk
me into ftill greater depths of wickednefs.
I was once roufed by the lofs of an intimate companion. We had agreed to go
on board a man of war (I think it was on
a *Sunday*;) but I providentially came too
late; the boat was overfet, and he and feveral others were drowned. I was invited

to

to the funeral of my play-fellow, and was exceedingly affected, to think that by a delay of a few minutes (which had much displeased and angered me till I saw the event) my life had been preserved. However this likewise was soon forgot. At another time the perusal of the *Family Instructor* put me upon a partial and transient reformation. In brief, though I cannot distinctly relate particulars, I think I took up and laid aside a religious profession three or four different times before I was sixteen years of age, but all this while my heart was insincere. I often saw a necessity of religion as a means of escaping hell, but I loved sin and was unwilling to forsake it. Instances of this I can remember, were frequent in the midst of all my forms; I was so strangely blind and stupid, that sometimes when I have been determined upon things, which I knew were sinful and contrary to my duty, I could not go on quietly, till I had first dispatched my ordinary task of prayer, in which I have grudged every moment of my time; and when this was finished, my conscience was in some measure pacified, and I could rush into folly with little remorse.

My

My laft reform was the moft remarkable both for degree and continuance. Of
this period, at leaft of fome part of it, I
may fay in the apoftle's words, " After the
" ftricteft fect of our religion, I lived a
" pharifee." I did every thing that might
be expected from a perfon entirely ignorant of God's righteoufnefs, and defirous
to eftablifh his own. I fpent the greateft
part of every day in reading the fcriptures,
meditation and prayer, I fafted often; I
even abftained from all animal food for
three months; I would hardly anfwer a
queftion, for fear of fpeaking an idle word.
I feemed to bemoan my former mifcar-
riages very earneftly, fometimes with tears.
In fhort, i became an afcetic, and endeavoured, fo far as my fituation would permit, to renounce fociety, that I might
avoid temptation. I continued in this ferious mood (I cannot give it a higher title)
for more than two years, without any confiderable breaking off. But it was a poor
religion; it left me in many refpects under the power of fin, and fo far as it prevailed, only tended to make me gloomy,
ftupid, unfociable, and ufelefs.

Such was the frame of my mind, when I
became acquainted with Lord *Shaftefbury*.

I faw

I faw the fecond volume of his *Charaateriftics*, in a petty fhop at *Middleburgh* in *Holland*. The title allured me to buy it, and the ftyle and manner gave me great pleafure in reading, efpecially the fecond piece, which his Lordfhip, with great propriety, has entitled a *Rhapfody*. Nothing could be more fuited to the romantic turn of my mind, than the addrefs of this pompous declamation; of the defign and tendency I was not aware; I thought the author a moft religious perfon, and that I had only to follow him, and be happy. Thus, with fine words and fair fpeeches, my fimple heart was beguiled. This book was always in my hand; I read it, till I could very nearly repeat the Rhapfody *verbatim* from beginning to end. No immediate effect followed, but it operated like a flow poifon, and prepared the way for all that followed.

This letter brings my hiftory down to *December*, 1742. I was then lately returned from a voyage, and my father not intending for the fea again, was thinking how to fettle me in the world; but I had little life or fpirit for bufinefs: I knew but little of men or things. I was fond of a vifionary fcheme of a contemplative life; a

medley

medley of religion, philofophy, and indolence; and was quite averfe to the thoughts
of an induftrious application to bufinefs.
At length a merchant in *Liverpool*, an intimate friend of my father (to whom, as
the inftrument of God's goodnefs, I have
fince been chiefly indebted for all my
earthly comforts) propofed to fend me for
fome years to *Jamaica*, and to charge himfelf with the care of my future fortune. I
confented to this, and every thing was
prepared for my voyage. I was upon the
point of fetting out the following week. In
the mean time, my father fent me on fome
bufinefs to a place a few miles beyond
Maidftone in *Kent*, and this little journey,
which was to have been only for three or
four days, occafioned a fudden and remarkable turn, which roufed me from the habitual indolence I had contracted, and gave
rife to the feries of uncommon difpenfations, of which you defire a more particular
account. So true it is, " that the way of
" man is not in himfelf, it is not in man
" that walketh to direct his fteps."

I am affectionately

Your's in the beft bonds.

JANUARY 13, 1763.

LETTER III.

DEAR SIR,

A FEW days before my intended journey into *Kent*, I received an invitation
to vifit a family in that county.— They
were diftant relations, but very intimate
friends of my dear mother: fhe died in
their houfe, but a coolnefs took place upon my father's fecond marriage, and I had
heard nothing of them for many years.
As my road lay within half a mile of their
houfe, I obtained my father's leave to call
on them. I was, however, very indifferent
about it, and fometimes thought of paffing
on : however I went: I was known at firft
fight, before I could tell my name, and
met with the kindeft reception, as the
child of a dear deceafed friend. My friends
had two daughters.— The eldeft (as I underftood fome years afterwards) had been
often confidered by her mother and mine,
as a future wife for me from the time of
her birth. I know indeed, that intimate
friends frequently amufe themfelves with
fuch diftant profpects for their children,
and

and that they mifcarry much oftener than fucceed. I do not fay that my mother predicted what was to happen, yet there was fomething remarkable in the manner of its taking place. All intercourfe between the families had been long broken off, I was going into a foreign country, and only called to pay a hafty vifit, and this I fhould not have thought of, but for a meffage received juft at that crifis (for I had not been invited at any time before). Thus the circumftances were precarious in the higheft degree, and the event was as extraordinary. Almoft at the firft fight of this girl (for fhe was then under fourteen) I was impreffed with an affection for her, which never abated or loft its influence a fingle moment in my heart from that hour. In degree, it actually equalled all that the writers of romance have imagined, in duration, it was unalterable. I foon loft all fenfe of religion, and became deaf to the remonftrances of confcience and prudence; but my regard for her was always the fame: and I may perhaps, venture to fay, that none of the fcenes of mifery and wickednefs I afterwards experienced, ever banifhed her a

fingle

single hour together, from my waking thoughts for the seven following years.

Give me leave, Sir, to reflect a little upon this unexpected incident, and to confider its influence upon my future life, and how far it was subservient to the views of Divine Providence concerning me, which seem to have been two-fold: that by being given up, for a while, to the consequences of my own wilfulnefs, and afterwards reclaimed by a high hand, my cafe, fo far as it should be known, might be both a warning and an encouragement to others.

In the firft place, hardly any thing lefs than this violent and commanding paffion would have been fufficient to awaken me from the dull melancholy habit I had contracted. I was almoft a mifanthrope, notwithftanding I fo much admired the pictures of virtue and benevolence as drawn by Lord *Shaftefbury*: but now my reluctance to active life was overpowered at once, and I was willing to be or to do any thing which might fubferve the accomplifhment of my wifhes at fome future time.

Farther, when I afterwards made ship-wreck of faith, hope, and confcience, my
love

love to this perfon was the only remaining principle, which in any degree fupplied their place; and the bear poffibility
of feeing her again was the only prefent
and obvious means of reftraining me from
the moft horrid defigns againft myfelf and
others.

But then the ill effects it brought upon
me counterbalanced thefe advantages.
The interval, ufually ftyled the time of
courtfhip, is indeed a pleafing part of life,
where there is a mutual affection, the confent of friends, a reafonable profpect as
to fettlement, and the whole is conducted
in a prudential manner, and in fubor-
dination to the will and fear of God.
When things are thus fituated, it is a
bleffing to be fufceptive of the tender
paffions; but when thefe concomitants
are wanting, what we call *love*, is the moft
tormenting paffion in *itfelf*, and the moft
deftructive in its *confequences*, that can be
named. And they were all wanting in
my cafe. I durft not mention it to her
friends, or to my own, nor indeed for a
confiderable time to herfelf, as I could
make no propofals: it remained as a dark
fire, locked up in my own breaft, which
gave me a conftant uneafinefs. By intro-

B 5

ducing an idolatrous regard to a creature, it greatly weakened my fenfe of religion, and made farther way for the entrance of infidel principles: and though it feemed to promife great things, as an incentive to diligence and activity in life; in reality, it performed nothing. I often formed mighty projects in my mind, of what I would willingly do or fuffer, for the fake of her I loved; yet, while I could have her company, I was incapable of forcing myfelf away, to improve opportunities that offered: ftill lefs could it do in regulating my manners. It did not prevent me from engaging in a long train of excefs and riot, utterly unworthy the honourable pretenfions I had formed. And though through the wonderful interpofition of Divine Goodnefs, the maze of my follies was at length unravelled, and my wifhes crowned in fuch a manner as overpaid my fufferings, yet, I am fure, I would not go through the fame feries of trouble again, to poffefs all the treafures of both the Indies. I have enlarged more than I intended on this point, as perhaps thefe papers may be ufeful to caution others againft indulging an ungovernable paffion, by my painful experience.

How

How often may fuch headftrong votaries be faid " To fow the wind, and to reap the whirlwind. "

My heart being now fixed and riveted to a particular object, I confidered every thing I was concerned with in a new light. I concluded it would be abfolutely impoffible to live at fuch a diftance as *Jamaica*, for a term of four or five years, and therefore determined at all events that I would not go. I could not bear either to acquaint my father with the true reafon, or to invent a falfe one; therefore, without taking any notice to him why I did fo, I ftayed three weeks inftead of three days in *Kent*, till I thought (as it proved) the opportunity would be loft, and the fhips failed. I then returned to *London*. I had highly difpleafed my father by this difobedience; but he was more eafily reconciled than I could have expected. In a little time I failed with a friend of his to *Venice*. In this voyage, I was expofed to the company and ill example of the common failors, among whom I ranked. Importunity, and opportunity, prefenting every day, I once more began to relax from the fobriety and order which I had obferved, in fome

degree

degree, for more than two years.—I was sometimes pierced with sharp convictions; but though I made a few faint efforts to stop, as I had done from several before; I did not, indeed, as yet turn out profligate, but I was making large strides towards a total apostacy from God. The most remarkable check and alarm, I received (and, for what I know, the last) was by a dream, which made a very strong, though not any abiding impression upon my mind.

The consideration of whom I am writing to, renders it needless for me, either to enter upon a discussion of the nature of dreams in general, or to make an apology for recording my own. Those who acknowledge scripture will allow, that there have been monitory and supernatural dreams, evident communications from heaven, either directing or foretelling future events : and those who are acquainted with the history and experience of the people of God, are well assured, that such intimations have not been totally withheld in any period down to the present times. Reason, far from contradicting this supposition, strongly pleads
for

for it, where the procefs of reafoning is
rightly underftood, and carefully purfued.
So that a late eminent writer*, who, I
prefume, is not generally charged with
enthufiafm, undertakes to prove, that the
phænomenon of dreaming is inexplicable
at leaft, if not abfolutely impoffible, without taking in the agency and intervention of fpiritual beings, to us invifible. I
would refer the incredulous to him. For
my own part, I can fay, without fcruple,
" The dream is certain, and the inter-
" pretation thereof fure." I am fure I
dreamed to the following effect, and I
cannot doubt, from what I have feen
fince, that it had a direct and eafy application to my own circumftances, to the
dangers, in which I was about to plunge
myfelf, and to the unmerited deliverance
and mercy, which God would be pleafed
to offer me in the time of my diftrefs.

Though I have wrote out a relation of
this dream more than once for others, it
has happened that I never referved a
copy; but the principal incidents are fo
deeply engraven in my memory, that I
believe I am not liable to any confiderable

* Baxter on the *Vis Inertiæ*.

variations in repeating the account. The scene prefented to my imagination, was the harbour of *Venice*, where we had lately been. I thought it was night, and my watch upon the deck, and that, as I was walking to and fro by myfelf, a perfon came to me, (I do not remember from whence) and brought me a ring, with an exprefs charge to keep it carefully; affuring me that while I preferved that ring, I fhould be happy and fuccefsful: but, if I loft, or parted with it, I muft expect nothing but trouble and mifery. I accepted the prefent and the terms willingly, not in the leaft doubting my own care to preferve it, and highly fatisfied to have my happinefs in my own keeping. I was engaged in thefe thoughts, when a fecond perfon came to me, and obferving the ring on my finger, took occafion to afk me fome queftions concerning it. I readily told him its virtues, and his anfwer expreffed a furprize at my weaknefs, in expecting fuch effects from a ring. I think he reafoned with me fome time upon the impoffibility of the thing, and at length urged me in direct terms, to throw it away. At firft, I was fhocked at the propofal, but his infinuations prevailed.

vailed. I began to reason and doubt myself, and at last plucked it off my finger,
and dropped it over the ship's side into
the water, which it had no sooner touched,
than I saw, the same instant, a terrible fire
burst out from a range of the mountains,
(a part of the *Alps*) which appeared at
some distance behind the city of *Venice*.
I saw the hills as distinct as if awake, and
they were all in flames. I perceived too
late my folly; and my tempter, with an
air of insult informed me, that all the
mercy God had in reserve for me, was
comprised in that ring, which I had wilfully thrown away. I understood that I
must now go with him to the burning
mountains, and that all the flames I saw
were kindled upon my account. I trem-
bled, and was in a great agony; so that
it was surprizing I did not then awake:
but my dream continued, and when I
thought myself upon the point of a con-
strained departure, and stood self-con-
demned, without plea or hope; suddenly,
either a third person, or the same who
brought the ring at first, came to me,
(I am not certain which) and demanded
the cause of my grief. I told him the
plain case, confessing that I had ruined
myself

myfelf wilfully, and deferved no pity.
He blamed my rafhnefs, and afked if I
fhould be wifer, fuppofing I had my ring
again. I could hardly anfwer to this;
for I thought it was gone beyond recall.
I believe, indeed, I had not time to anfwer, before I faw this unexpected friend
go down under the water, juft in the fpot
where I had dropped it, and he foon returned, bringing the ring with him. The
moment he came on board, the flames
in the mountains were extinguifhed, and
my feducer left me. Then was " the
" prey taken from the hand of the mighty,
" and the lawful captive delivered " My
fears were at an end, and with joy and
gratitude I approached my kind deliverer
to receive the ring again, but he refufed
to return it, and fpoke to this effect:
" If you fhould be entrufted with this
" ring again, you would very foon bring
" yourfelf into the fame diftrefs; you are
" not able to keep it, but I will preferve
" it for you, and whenever it is needful,
" will produce it in your behalf."——
Upon this I awoke, in a ftate of mind not
to be defcribed: I could hardly eat, or
fleep, or tranfact my neceffary bufinefs
for two or three days: but the impreffion

foon

foon wore off, and in a little time I totally
forgot it; and I think it hardly occured
to my mind again, till feveral years afterwards. It will appear, in the courfe of
thefe papers, that a time came, when I
found myfelf in circumftances very nearly
refembling thofe fuggefted by this extraordinary dream, when I ftood helplefs
and hopelefs upon the brink of an awful
eternity: and I doubt not but, had the
eyes of my mind been then opened, I
fhould have feen my grand enemy, who
had feduced me, wilfully to renounce and
caft away my religious profeffion, and to
involve myfelf in the moft complicated
crimes; I fay, I fhould probably have
feen him pleafed with my agonies, and
waiting for a permiffion, to feize and bear
away my foul to this place of torment. I
fhould perhaps have feen likewife, that
Jefus, whom I had perfecuted and defied,
rebuking the adverfary, challenging me
for his own, as a brand plucked out of
the fire, and faying, " Deliver me from
" going down into the pit; I have found
" a ranfom." However, though I faw
not thefe things, I found the benefit; I
obtained mercy. The Lord anfwered for
me in the day of my diftrefs; and, bleffed
be

be his name, he who reftored the ring,
(or what was fignified by it) vouchfafes
to keep it. O what an unfpeakable comfort is this, that I am not in mine own
keeping. " The Lord is my fhepherd :"
I have been able to truft mine all in his
hands, and I know in whom I have believed. Satan ftill defires to have me,
that he might fift me as wheat; but my
Saviour has prayed for me, that my faith
may not fail. Here is my fecurity and
power, a bulwark, againft which the
gates of hell cannot prevail. But for
this, many a time and often (if poffible)
I fhould have ruined myfelf, fince my firft
deliverance, nay, I fhould fall, and ftum-
ble, and perifh ftill, after all that the
Lord has done for me, if his faithfulnefs
was not engaged in my behalf, to be my
fun and fhield even unto death. — " Blefs
the Lord, O my foul !"

Nothing very remarkable occurred in
the following part of that voyage. I returned home in *December* 1743, and foon
after repeated my vifit to *Kent*, where I
protracted my ftay in the fame imprudent
manner I had done before, which again
difappointed my father's defigns in my
favour, and almoft provoked him to dif-

own

own me. Before any thing fuitable offered
again, I was impreffed (owing entirely
to my own thoughtlefs conduct, which
was all of a piece) and put on board a
tender; it was a critical juncture, when
the *French* fleets were hovering upon our
coaft, fo that my father was incapable to
procure my releafe. In a few days I was
fent on board the *Harwich* man of war, at
the *Nore.* I entered here upon quite a
new fcene of life, and endured much hardfhip for about a month. My father was
then willing that I fhould remain in the
navy, as a war was daily expected, and
procured me a recommendation to the
Captain, who took me upon the quarter
deck as a midfhipman. I had now an
eafy life, as to externals, and might have
gained refpect, but my mind was unfettled, and my behaviour very indifferent.
I here met with companions who completed the ruin of my principles; and
though I affected to talk of virtue, and
was not fo outwardly abandoned as afterwards, yet my delight and habitual practice was wickednefs: my chief intimate
was a perfon of exceeding good natural
talents, and much obfervation; he was
the greateft mafter of what is called the

free-

free-thinking fcheme, I remember to have
met with, and knew how to infinuate his
fentiments in the moft plaufible way.—
And his zeal was equal to his addrefs; he
could hardly have laboured more in the
caufe, if he had expected to gain heaven
by it. Allow me to add, while I think
of it, that this man, whom I honoured
as my mafter, and whofe practice I adopted
fo eagerly, perifhed in the fame way as
I expected to have done. I have been
told, that he was overtaken in a voyage
from *Lifbon* with a violent ftorm: the
veffel and people efcaped, but a great fea
broke on board and fwept him into eternity.—Thus the Lord fpares or punifhes,
according to his fovereign pleafure! But
to return:—I was fond of his company,
and having myfelf a fmattering of books,
was eager enough to fhew my reading.
He foon perceived my cafe, that I had
not wholly broke through the reftraints
of confcience, and therefore did not
fhock me at firft with too broad intimations of his defign, he rather, as I
thought, fpoke favourably of religion;
but when he had gained my confidence,
he began to fpeak plainer; and perceiving
my ignorant attachment to the *Characte-
riftics,*

riſtics he joined iſſue with me upon that book, and convinced me that I had never understood it. In a word, he ſo plied me with objections and arguments, that my depraved heart was ſoon gained, and I entered into his plan with all my ſpirit. Thus, like an unwary ſailor, who quits his port juſt before a riſing ſtorm, I renounced the hopes and comforts of the goſpel at the very time when every other comfort was about to fail me.

In *December* 1744, the *Harwich* was in the *Downs*, bound to the *Eaſt Indies*. The Captain gave me liberty to go on ſhore for a day; but without conſulting prudence, or regarding conſequences, I took horſe, and followed the dictates of my reſtleſs paſſion, I went to take a laſt leave of her I loved. I had little ſatisfaction in the interview, as I was ſenſible that I was taking pains to multiply my own troubles. The ſhort time I could ſtay paſſed like a dream, and on new year's day, 1745, I took my leave to return to the ſhip. The Captain was prevailed on to excuſe my abſence, but this raſh ſtep (eſpecially as it was not the firſt liberty of the kind I had taken) highly diſpleaſed him, and loſt me his favour, which I never recovered.

At

At length we failed from *Spithead* with
a very large fleet. We put into *Torbay*
with a change of wind; but it returning
fair again, we failed the next day. Several of our fleet were loft in attempting to
leave that place; but the following night
the whole fleet was greatly endangered
upon the coaft of *Cornwall*, by a ftorm
from the fouthward. The darknefs of
the night and the number of the veffels,
occafioned much confufion and damage.
Our fhip, though feveral times in immi-
nent danger of being run down by other
veffels, efcaped unhurt, but many fuffered
much, particularly the *Admiral*. This
occafioned our putting back to *Plymouth*.

While we lay at *Plymouth*, I heard that
my father, who had intereft in fome of
the fhips lately loft, was come down to
Torbay. He had a connection at that time
with the *African* company. I thought
if I could get to him, he might eafily in-
troduce me into that fervice, which would
be better than purfuing a long uncertain
voyage to the *Eaft Indies*. It was a maxim
with me, in thofe unhappy days, *never
to deliberate*; the thought hardly occurred
to me but I was refolved I would leave
the fhip at all events : I did fo, and in the
wrongeft

wrongeft manner poffible. I was fent one
day in the boat, to take care that none of
the people deferted; but I betrayed my
truft, and went off myfelf. I knew not
what road to take, and durft not afk; for
fear of being fufpected; yet having fome
general idea of the country, I gueffed
right, and, when I had travelled fome
miles, I found, upon inquiry, that I was
on the road to *Dartmouth*. All went
fmoothly that day, and part of the next: I
walked apace, and expected to have been
with my father in about two hours, when I
was met by a fmall party of foldiers; I
could not avoid or deceive them. They
brought me back to *Plymouth*; I walked
through the ftreets guarded like a felon.——
My heart was full of indignation, fhame,
and fear.——I was confined two days in the
guard-houfe, then fent on board my fhip,
kept a-while in irons, then publicly ftrip-
ped and whipped, after which I was de-
graded from my office, and all my former
companions forbidden to fhew me the leaft
favour, or even to fpeak to me.——As
midfhipman, I had been entitled to fome
command, which (being fufficiently haughty
and vain) I had not been backward to
exert.——I was now in my turn brought
                                    down

down to a level with the loweft, and expofed to the infults of all.

And as my prefent fituation was un-
comfortable, my future profpects were
ftill worfe; the evils I fuffered were likely
to grow heavier every day. While my
cataftrophe was recent, the officers and
my quondam brethren were fomething difpofed to fcreen me from ill ufage, but,
during the little time I remained with
them afterwards, I found them cool very
faft in their endeavours to protect me.
Indeed they could not avoid it without
running a great rifk of fharing with me: for
the Captain, though in general a humane
man, who behaved very well to the fhip's
company, was almoft implacable in his
refentment. when he had been greatly of-
fended, and took feveral occafions to fhew
himfelf fo to me, and the voyage was expected to be (as it proved) for five years.
Yet I think nothing I either felt or feared
diftreffed me fo much, as to fee myfelf
thus forcibly torn away from the object
of my affections, under a great improba-
bility of feeing her again, and a much
greater, of returning in fuch a manner as
would give me hopes of feeing her mine.
Thus I was as miferable on all hands as
                                        could

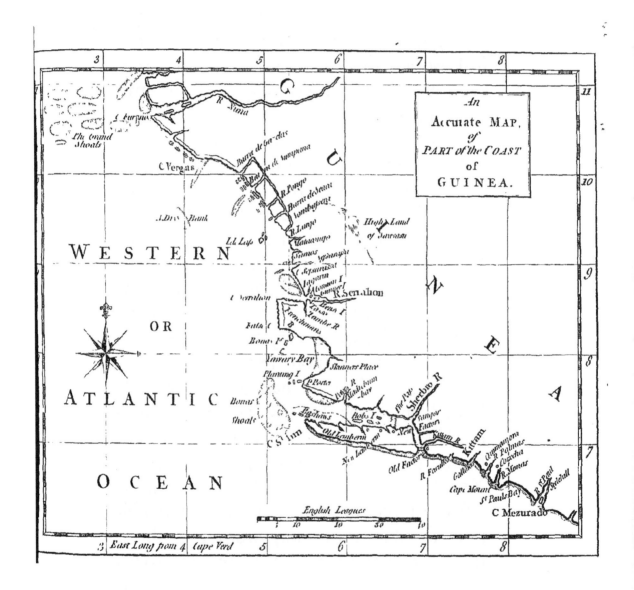

An Accurate Map, of PART of the COAST of GUINEA.

could well be imagined. My breaft was
filled with the moft excruciating pàffions,
eager defire, bitter rage, and black defpair.—Every hour expofed me to fome
new infult and hardfhip, with no hope of
relief or mitigation, no friend to take my
part, or to liften to my complaint. Whether I looked inward or outward, I could
perceive nothing but darknefs and mifery.
I think no cafe, except that of a confcience,
wounded by the wrath of God, could be
more dreadful than mine; I cannot exprefs
with what wifhfulnefs and regret, I caft my
laft looks upon the *Englifh* fhore, I kept
my eyes fixed upon it till, the fhip's diftance increafing, it fenfibly difappeared;
and when I could fee it no longer, I was
tempted to throw myfelf into the fea,
which (according to the wicked fyftem I
had adopted) would put a period to all
my forrows at once. But the fecret hand
of God reftrained me. Help me to praife
him, dear Sir, for his wonderful goodnefs
to the moft unworthy of all his creatures.

I am

Your moft obliged fervant.

January 15, 1753.

C   LETTER

LETTER IV.

DEAR SIR,

THOUGH I defired your inftructions as to the manner and extent of thefe memoirs, I began to write before I received them, and had almoft finifhed the preceding fheet when your favour of the eleventh came to hand. I fhall find another occafion to acknowledge my fenfe of your kind expreffions of friendfhip, which I pray the Lord, I may never give you caufe to repent or withdraw; at prefent I fhall confine myfelf to what more particularly relates to the tafk affigned me. I fhall obey you, Sir, in taking notice of the little incidents you recall to my memory, and of otheis of the like nature, which, without your direction, I fhould have thought too trivial, and too much my own to deferve mentioning. When I began the eight letters, I intended to fay no more of myfelf than might be neceffary to illuftrate the wonders of Divine
Providence

Providence and grace in the leading turns of my life, but I account your judgment a fufficient warrant for enlarging my plan.

Amongſt other things, you defired a more explicit account of the ſtate and progreſs of my courtſhip, as it is ufually phraſed. This was the point in which I thought it eſpecially became me to be very brief; but I ſubmit to you; and this feems a proper place to refume it, by telling you how it ſtood at the time of my leaving *England*. When my inclinations firſt diſcovered themſelves, both parties were ſo young, that no one but myſelf confidered it in a ferious view. It ferved for tea-table talk amongſt our friends, and nothing farther was expected from it. But afterwards, when my paffion ſeemed to have abiding effects, ſo that in an interval of two years it was not at all abated, and eſpecially as it occafioned me to act without any regard to prudence or intereſt, or my father's defigns, and as there was a coolneſs between him and the family, her parents began to confider it as a matter of confequence, and when I took my laſt leave of them, her mother, at the fame time ſhe expreſſed the moſt tender

affection

affection for me, as if I had been her own
child, told me, That though she had no
objections to make, upon a supposition
that, at a matuier age, there should be
a probability of our engaging upon a
prudent profpect, yet, as things then stood,
she thought herself obliged to interfere;
and therefore desired I would no more
think of returning to their house (unless
her daughter was from home) till such
time as I could either prevail with myfelf entirely to give up my pretensions,
or could assure her that I had my father's
exprefs consent to go on.   Much depended on Mrs. N******'s part in this affair, it was something difficult; but though
she was young, gay, and quite unpractifed
in such matteis, she was directed to a happy medium.   A positive encouragement,
or an absolute iefufal, would have been
attended with equal, though diffeient dif-
advantages.   But without much studying
about it, I found her always upon her
guard. she had penetration to fee her
absolute power over me, and prudence
to make a proper ufe of it; she would
neither undeistand my hints, nor give
me room to come to a direct explanation.
She has faid fince that from the firft dif-

covery

covery of my regard, and long before the thought was agreeable to her, fhe had of-ten an unaccountable impreffion upon her mind that fooner or later fhe fhould be mine. Upon thefe terms we parted.

I now return to my voyage. During our paffage to *Madeira,* I was a prey to the moft gloomy thoughts. Though I had well deferved all I met with, and the Captain might have been juftified if he had carried his refentment ftill farther; yet my pride at that time fuggefted that I had been grofsly injured, and this fo far wrought upon my wicked heart, that I actually formed defigns againft his life, and this was one reafon that made me willing to piolong my own. I was fome-times divided between the two, not thinking it practicable to effect both. The Lord had now to appearance given me up to judicial hardnefs; I was capable of any thing. I had not the leaft fear of God before my eyes, nor (fo far as I re-member) the leaft fenfibility of confcience. I was poffeffed of fo ftrong a fpirit of de-lufion that I believed my own lie, and was firmly perfuaded that after death I fhould ceafe to be.—Yet the Lord pre-ferved me!—Some intervals of fober re-

flection

flection would at times take place: when
I have chosen death rather than life, a ray
of hope would come in (though there
was little probability for such a hope)
that I should yet see better days, that I
might again return to *England*, and have
my wishes crowned, if I did not wilfully
throw myself away. In a word, my love to
Mrs. N****** was now the only restraint
I had left; though I neither feared God,
nor regarded men, I could not bear that
she should think meanly of me, when I was
dead. As in the outward concerns of life,
the weakest means are often employed by
Divine Providence to produce great effects, beyond their common influence, (as
when a disease, for instance, has been removed by a fright) as I found it then:
this single thought, which had not re-
strained me from a thousand smaller evils,
proved my only and effectual barrier
against the greatest and most fatal temptations. How long I could have supported
this conflict, or what, humanely speaking,
would have been the consequence of my
continuing in that situation, I cannot say;
but the Lord, whom I little thought of,
knew my danger, and was providing for
my deliverance.

Two

Two things I had determined when at *Plymouth*, that I would *not* go to *India*, and that I *would* go to *Guinea*, and such indeed, was the Lord's will concerning me; but they were to be accomplished in his way, not in my own. We had been now at *Madeira* some time; the business of the fleet was completed, and we were to sail the following day. On that memorable morning I was late in bed, and had slept longer, but that one of the midshipmen (an old companion) came down, and, between jest and earnest, bid me rise; and, as I did not immediately comply, he cut down the hammock or bed in which I lay, which forced me to dress myself. I was very angry, but durst not resent it. I was little aware how much his caprice affected me, and that this person, who had no design in what he did, was the messenger of God's providence. I said little, but went upon deck, where I that moment saw a man putting his clothes in a boat, who told me he was going to leave us. Upon inquiring, I was informed that two men from a *Guinea* ship, which lay near us, had entered on board the *Harwich*, and that the Commodore (the present Sir *George Po-*

C 4

cock) had ordered the Captain to fend
two others in their room. My heart instantly burned like fire.—I begged the
boat might be detained a few minutes;
I ran to the lieutenants, and entreated
them to intercede with the Captain that
I might be difmiffed upon this occafion.
Though I had been formerly upon ill
terms with thefe officers, and had difo-
bliged them all in their turns: yet they had
pitied my cafe, and were ready to ferve
me now. The Captain, who, when we
were at *Plymouth*, had refufed to exchange
me, though at the requeft of Admiral
Medley, was now eafily prevailed on. I
believe in little more than half an hour
from my being afleep in my bed, I faw
myfelf difcharged, and fafe on board another fhip. This was one of the many
critical turns of my life, in which the Lord
was pleafed to difplay his providence and
care, by caufing many unexpected circumftances to concur in almoft an inftant
of time. Thefe fudden opportunities
were feveral times repeated: each of
them brought me into an entire new fcene
of action; and they were ufually delayed
to almoft the laft moment, in which they
could have taken place.

The

The ship I went on board was bound
to *Sierra Leon,* and the adjacent parts of
what is called the *Windward Coast of Africa.*
The commander I found was acquaint-
ed with my father; he received me very
kindly, and made fair professions of
assistance; and, I believe he would have
been my friend; but, without making the
least advantage of former mistakes and
troubles, I pursued the same course;
nay, if possible, I acted much worse. On
board the *Harwich,* though my principles
were totally corrupted, yet, as upon my
first going there I was in some degree
staid and serious, the remembrance of this
made me ashamed of breaking out in
that notorious manner I could otherwise
have indulged. But, now entering amongst
strangers, I could appear without disguise;
and I well remember, that while I was
passing from the one ship to the other,
this was one reason why I rejoiced in the
exchange, and one reflection I made upon
the occasion, viz. " That I now might
" be as abandoned as I pleased, without
" any controul:" and, from this time, I
was exceedingly vile indeed, little, if any
thing short of that animated description
of an almost irrecoverable state, which we

have

have in 2 *Peter* ii. 14. I not only finned with a high hand myfelf, but made it my ftudy to tempt and feduce others upon every occafion: nay, I eagerly fought occafion fometimes to my own hazard and hurt. One natural confequence of this carriage was, a lofs of the favour of my new captain; not that he was at all religious or difliked my wickednefs, any further than it affected his intereft; but I became carelefs and difobedient; I did not pleafe him, becaufe I did not intend it; and, as he was a man of an odd temper likewife, we the more eafily difagreed. Befides, I had a little of that unlucky wit which can do little more than multiply troubles and enemies to its poffeffor; and upon fome imagined affront, I made a fong in which I ridiculed his fhip, his defigns, and his perfon, and foon taught it to the whole fhip's company. Such was the ungrateful return I made for his offers of friendfhip and protection. I had mentioned no names, but the allufion was plain, and he was no ftranger either to the intention or the author.——I fhall fay no more of this part of my ftory; let it be buried in eternal filence. But let me not be filent from the praife of that

grace,

grace which could pardon, that blood which could expiate such sins as mine; yea, " the Ethiopian may change his skin, and the leopard his spots," since I who was the willing slave of every evil, possessed with a legion of unclean spirits, have been spared, and saved, and changed, to stand as a monument of his almighty power for ever.

Thus I went on for about six months, by which time the ship was preparing to leave the coast. A few days before she sailed the Captain died. I was not upon much better terms with his mate, who now succeeded to the command, and had upon some occasion, treated me ill: I made no doubt, but, if I went with him to the *West Indies*, he would put me on board a man of war; and this, from what I had known already, was more dreadful to me than death. To avoid it, I determined to remain in *Africa*, and amused myself with many golden dreams, that here I should find an opportunity of improving my fortune.

There are still upon that part of the coast, a few white men settled (and there were many more at the time I was first there) whose business it was to purchase

slaves,

flaves, &c. in the rivers and country adjacent, and fell them to the fhips at an
advanced price. One of thefe, who at
firft landed in my indigent circumftances,
had acquired confiderable wealth : he had
lately been in *England*, and was returning
in the veffel I was in, of which he owned
a quarter part. His example impreffed
me with hopes of the fame fuccefs; and
upon condition of entering into his fervice,
I obtained my difcharge. I had not the
precaution to make any terms, but trufted
to his generofity. I received no compen-
fation for my time on board the fhip, but
a bill upon the owners in *England* which
was never paid, for they failed before my
return. The day the veffel failed I landed
upon the ifland of *Beñanoes*, with little more
than the clothes upon my back, as if I had
efcaped fhipwreck.

I am, dear Sir,

Yours, &c.

LETTER

LETTER V.

DEAR SIR,

THERE seems an important instruction, and of frequent use, in these words of our dear Lord, " Mine hour is not yet come." The two following years, of which I am now to give some account, will seem as an absolute blank in a very short life: but as the Lord's hour of grace was not yet come, and I was to have still deeper experience of the dreadful state of the heart of man, when left to itself; I have seen frequent cause since, to admire the mercy of the Lord in banishing me to those distant parts, and almost excluding me from human society, at a time when I was big with mischief, and, like one infected with a pestilence, was capable of spreading a taint wherever I went. Had my affairs taken a different turn, had I succeeded in my designs, and remained in *England*, my sad story would probably have been worse——

Worse

Worfe in myfelf, indeed, I could have hardly been; but my wickednefs would have had greater fcope; I might have been very hurtful to others, and multi-plied irreparable evils. But the Lord wifely placed me where I could do little harm. The few I had to converfe with were too much like myfelf, and I was foon brought into fuch abject circum-ftances, that I was too low to have any influence. I was rather fhunned and de-fpifed, than imitated; there being few even of the negroes themfelves, (during the firft year of my refidence among them) but thought themfelves too good to fpeak to me. I was as yet an " outcaft lying in my blood," (*Ezek.* xvi.) and, to all appearance, expofed to perifh. — But the Lord beheld me with mercy — he did not ftrike me to hell, as I juftly deferved; " he paffed by me when I was in my blood, and bid me live." But the appointed time for the manifeftation of his love, to cover all my iniquities with the robe of his righteoufnefs, and to admit me to the privileges of his children, was, not till long afterwards, yet even now he bid me *live*, and I can only afcribe it to his fecret up-holding power, that what I fuffered in a

part

part of this interval, did not bereave me either of my life or senses; yet as by these sufferings the force of my evil example and inclinations was lessened, I have reason to account them amongst my mercies.

It may not, perhaps, be amiss to digress for a few lines, and give you a very brief sketch of the geography of the circuit I was now confined to, especially as I may have frequent occasion to refer to places I shall now mention; for my trade afterwards, when the Lord gave me to see better days, was chiefly to the same places, and with the same persons, where and by whom I had been considered as upon a level with their meanest slaves. From *Cape de Verd*, the most western point of *Africa*, to *Cape Mount*, the whole coast is full of rivers: the principal are *Gambia*, *Rio Grande*, *Sierra Leon*, and *Sherbro*. Of the former, as it is well known, and I was never there, I need say nothing. The *Rio Grande* (like the *Nile*) divides into many branches near the sea. On the most northerly, called *Cacheo*, the *Portuguese* have a settlement. The most southern branch, known by the name of *Rio Nuna*, is, or was, the usual boundary of the white

white men's trade northward. *Sierra Leon*
is a mountainous peninfula, uninhabited,
and I believe inacceffible, upon account
of the thick woods, excepting thofe parts
which lie near the water. The river is
large and navigable. From hence about
twelve leagues to the fouth-eaft, are three
contiguous iflands, called the *Benanoes*,
about twenty miles in circuit; this was
about the centre of the white men's refidence. Seven leagues farther the fame
way, lie the *Plantanes*, three fmall iflands,
two miles diftant from the continent at
the point which form one fide of the
Sherbro. This river is more properly a
found, running within a long ifland, and
receiving the confluence of feveral large
rivers, " *rivers unknown to fong*," but far
more deeply engraven in my remembrance, than the *Po* or *Tyber*. The
fouthern-moft of thefe has a very peculiar courfe, almoft parallel to the coaft;
fo that in tracing it a great many leagues
upwards, it will feldom lead one above
three miles, and fometimes not more than
half a mile from the fea fhore. Indeed I
know not, but that all thefe rivers may
have communications with each other,
and with the fea in many places, which I
have

have not remarked. If you caft your eyes upon a large map of *Africa*, while you are reading this, you will have a general idea of the country I was in; for though the maps are very incorrect, moft of the places I have mentioned are inferted, and in the fame order as I have named them.

My new mafter had formerly refided near *Cape Mount*, but he now fettled at the *Plantanes*, upon the largeft, of the three iflands. It is a low fandy ifland, about two miles in circumference, and almoft covered with palm-trees. We immediately began to build a houfe, and to enter upon trade. I had now fome defire to retrieve my loft time, and to exert diligence in what was before me; and he was a man with whom I might have lived tolerably well, if he had not been foon influenced againft me: but he was much under the direction of a black woman, who lived with him as a wife. She was a perfon of fome confequence in her own country; and he owed his fiift rife to her intereft. This woman (I know not for what reafon) was ftrangely prejudiced againft me from the firft; and what made it ftill worfe for me, was a fevere fit of

illnefs,

illnefs, which attacked me very foon before I had opportunity to fhew what I,
could or would do in his fervice. I was
fick when he failed in a fhalop, to *Rio
Nuna*, and he left me in her hands. At
firft I was taken fome care off; but, as I
did not recover very foon, fhe grew weary,
and entirely neglected me. I had fometimes not a little difficulty to procure a
diaught of cold water, when burning
with a fever. My bed was a mat, fpread
upon a board or cheft, and a log of wood
my pillow. When my favour left me,
and my appetite returned, I would gladly
have eaten, but there was no one gave
unto me. She lived in plenty herfelf,
but hardly allowed me fufficient to fuftain life, except now and then, when in
the higheft good humour, fhe would
fend me victuals in her own plate, after
fhe had dined, and this (fo greatly was
my pride humbled) I received with thanks
and eagernefs as the moft needy beggar
does an alms. Once, I well remember,
I was called to receive this bounty fiom
her own hand, but, being exceedingly
weak and feeble, I dropped the plate.
Thofe who live in plenty can hardly conceive how this lofs touched me; but fhe
had

had the cruelty to laugh at my difappointment; and though the table was covered, with difhes (for fhe lived much in the *European* manner) fhe refufed to give me any more. My diftrefs has been at times fo great, as to compel me to go, by night, and pull up roots in the plantation, (though at the rifk of being punifhed as a thief) which I have eaten raw upon the fpot, for fear of difcovery. The roots I fpeak of are very wholefome food, when boiled or roafted, but as unfit to be eaten raw, in any quantity, as a potatoe. The confequence of this diet, which, after the firft experiment, I always expected, and feldom miffed, was the fame as if I had taken *tartar emetic*; fo that I have often returned as empty as I went: yet neceffity urged me to repeat the trial feveral times. I have fometimes been relieved by ftrangers; nay, even by the flaves in the chain, who have fecretly brought me victuals (for they durft not be feen to do it) from their own flender pittance. Next to preffing want, nothing fits harder upon the mind than *fcorn* and *contempt*, and of this likewife I had an abundant meafure. When I was very flowly recovering, this woman would

fome-

fometimes pay me a vifit, not to pity or relieve, but to infult me. She would call me worthlefs and indolent, and compel me to walk, which, when I could hardly do, fhe would fet her attendants to mimic my motion, to clap their hands, laugh, throw limes at me; or, if they chofe, to throw ftones (as I think was the cafe once or twice) they were not rebuked: but, in general, though all who depended on her favour muft join in her treatment, yet, when fhe was out of fight, I was rather pitied than fcorned by the meaneft of her flaves. At length my mafter returned from his voyage; I complained of ill ufage, but he could not believe me; and, as I did it in her hearing, I fared no better for it. But in his fecond voyage he took me with him. We did pretty well for a while, till a brother trader he met in the river, perfuaded him that I was unfaithful, and ftole his goods in the night, or when he was on fhore. This was almoft the only vice I could not be juftly charged with: the only remains of a good education I could boaft of, was what is commonly called *honefty:* and, as far as he had entrufted me, I had been always true; and though my great diftrefs

trefs might, in some measure, have excused
it, I never once thought of defrauding
him in the smallest matter. However, the
charge was believed, and I condemned
without evidence. From that time *he*
likewise used me very hardly; whenever
he left the vessel I was locked upon deck,
with a pint of rice for my day's allowance;
and if he staid longer, I had no relief till
his return. Indeed, I believe I should
have been nearly starved, but for an
opportunity of catching fish sometimes.
When fowls were killed for his own use, I
seldom was allowed any part but the en-
trails, to bait my hooks with: and, at what
we call *slack water*, that is, about the changing of the tides, when the current was still
I used generally to fish (for at other times
it was not practicable) and I very often
succeeded. If I saw a fish upon my hook,
my joy was little less than any other person may have found, in the accomplishment of the scheme he had most at heart.
Such a fish, hastily broiled, or rather half
burnt, without sauce, salt, or bread, has
afforded me a delicious meal. If I caught
none, I might, if I could, sleep away my
hunger till the next return of *slack water*,
and then try again. Nor did I suffer less
from

from the inclemency of the weather and the want of clothes. The rainy feafon was now advancing; my whole fuit was a fhirt, a pair of trowfers, a cotton handkerchief inftead of a cap, and a cotton cloth about two yards long, to fupply the want of upper garments: and thus accoutered, I have been expofed for twenty, thirty, perhaps near forty hours together, in inceffant rains, accompanied with ftrong gales of wind, without the leaft fhelter, when my mafter was on fhore. I feel to this day fome faint returns of the violent pains I then contracted. The exceffive cold and wet I endured in that voyage, and fo foon after I had recovered from a long ficknefs quite bioke my conftitution and my fpirits; the latter were foon reftored, but the effects of the former ftill remain with me, as a needful memento of the fervice and the wages of fin.

In about two months we returned, and then the reft of the time I remained with him was chiefly fpent at the *Plantanes*, under the fame regimen as I have already mentioned. My haughty heart was now brought down, not to a wholefome repentance, not to the language of the prodigal; this was far from me; but my fpirits were
funk;

funk; I loft all refolution, and almoft all reflection. I had loft the fiercenefs which fired me when on board the *Harwich*, and which made me capable of the moft defperate attempts; but I was no further changed than a tiger, tamed by hunger—remove the occafion and he will be as wild as ever.

One thing, though ftrange, is moft true. Though deftitute of food and clothing, depreffed to a degree beyond common wretchednefs, I could fometimes collect my mind to mathematical ftudies. I had bought *Barrow's Euclid* at *Plymouth*; it was the only volume I brought on fhore; it was always with me, and I ufed to take it to remote corners of the ifland by the fea fide, and draw my *diagrams* with a long ftick upon the fand. Thus I often beguiled my forrows, and almoft forgot my feeling:—and thus, without any other affiftance, I made myfelf in a good meafure, mafter of the firft fix books of *Euclid*.

I am

Your's as before.

JANUARY 17, 1763.

LETTER

LETTER VI.

DEAR SIR,

THERE is much piety and spirit in the grateful acknowledgment of *Jacob*, " with my ftaff I paffed this *Jordan*, and now I am become two bands." They are words which ought to affect me with a peculiar emotion. I remember that fome of thofe mournful days, to which my laft letter refers, I was bufied in planting fome *lime* or *lemon trees*. The plants I put in the ground were no longer than a young *goofeberry* bufh, my mafter and his miftrefs paffing by the place, ftopped a while to look at me; at laft, " Who " knows," fays he, " who knows but by " the time thefe trees grow up and bear, " you may go home to *England*, obtain " the command of a fhip, and return to " reap the fruits of your labours; we fee " ftrange things fometimes happen."— This, as he intended it, was a cutting farcafm. I believe he thought it full as pro-

bable

bable that I fhould live to be king of *Po-land*, yet it proved a prediction, and they (one of them at leaft) lived to fee me return from *England*, in the capacity he had mentioned, and pluck fome of the firft limes from thofe very trees. How can I proceed in my relation, till I raife a monument to the divine goodnefs, by comparing the circumftances in which the Lord has fince placed me, with what I was at that time! Had you feen me, Sir, then go fo penfive and folitary in the dead of night to wafh my one fhirt upon the rocks, and afterwards put it on wet, that it might dry upon my back, while I flept; had you feen me fo poor a figure, that when a fhip's boat came to the ifland, fhame often conftrained me to hide myfelf in the woods, from the fight of ftrangers; efpecially, had you known that my conduct, principles and heart were ftill darker than my outward condition—how little would you have imagined, that one, who fo fully anfwered to the* ςυγητοι και μισϑντες of the apoftle, was referved to be fo peculiar an inftance of the providential care, and exuberant goodnefs of

* Hateful, and hating one another.

D   God.

God. There was, at that time, but one
earneft defire in my heart, which was not
contrary and fhocking both to religion
and reafon; that *one* defiie, though my
vile licentious life rendered me peculiarly
unworthy of fuccefs, and though a thoufand difficulties feemed to render it impoffible, the Lord was pleafed to gratify.
But this favour, though great, and greatly
prized, was a fmall thing compared to
the bleffings of his grace : he fpared me,
to give me the " knowledge of himfelf,
in the perfon of Jefus Chrift," in love
to my foul he delivered me from the
pit of corruption, and caft all my aggravated fins behind his back. He brought
my feet into the paths of peace.—This is
indeed the chief aiticle, but it is not the
whole. When he made me acceptable
to himfelf in the beloved, he gave me
favour in the fight of others. He raifed
me new friends, protected and guided
me through a long feiies of dangers, and
crowned every day with repeated mercies.
To him I owe it that I am ftill alive, and
that I am not ftill living in hunger, and
in thiift, and in nakednefs, and the want
of all things : into that ftate I brought myfelf, but it was he who delivered me. He
has

has given me an eafy fituation in life, fome experimental knowledge of his gofpel, a large acquaintance amongft his people, a friendfhip and correfpondence with feveral of his moft honoured fervants.—But it is as difficult to enumerate my prefent advantages, as it is fully to defcribe the evils and miferies of the preceding contraft.

I know not exactly how long things continued with me thus, but I believe near a twelvemonth. In this interval, I wrote two or three times to my father; I gave him an account of my condition, and defired his affiftance, intimating at the fame time, that I had refolved not to return to *England*, unlefs he was pleafed to fend for me; I have likewife letters by me, wrote to Mrs. ―――― in that difmal period; fo that at the loweft ebb, it feems I ftill retained a hope of feeing her again. My father applied to his friend in *Liver-pool*, of whom I have fpoken before, who gave orders accordingly to a captain of his, who was then fitting out for *Gambia* and *Sierra Leon*.

Some time within the year, as I have faid, I obtained my mafter's confent to live with another trader, who dwelt upon

the

the fame ifland. Without his confent I
could not be taken, and he was unwilling
to do it fooner, but it was then brought
about. This was an alteration much to
my advantage; I was foon decently clo-
thed, lived in plenty, was confidered as a
companion, and trufted with the care of
all his domeftic effects which were to the
amount of fome thoufand pounds. This
man had feveral factories and white fervants in different places, particularly one
in *Kittam*, the river I fpoke of which
runs fo near along the fea coaft. I was
foon appointed to go there, where I had
a fhare in the management of bufinefs,
jointly with another of his fervants: we
lived as we pleafed, bufinefs flourifhed,
and our employer was fatisfied. Here
I began to be wretch enough to think
myfelf *happy*. There is a fignificant phrafe
frequently ufed in thofe parts, that fuch
a white man is grown *black*. It does not
intend an alteration of complexion, but
difpofition. I have known feveral, who,
fettling in *Africa* after the age of thirty, or
forty, have, at that time of life been gradually affimilated to the tempers, cuftoms,
and ceremonies of the natives, fo far as
to prefer that country to *England*; they
have

have even become dupes to all the pretended charms, necromances, amulets, and divinations of the blinded negroes, and put more truft in fuch things than the wifer fort among the natives. A part of this fpirit of infatuation was growing upon me (in time perhaps I might have yielded to the whole); I entered into clofer engagements with the inhabitants, and fhould have lived and died a wretch amongft them, if the Lord had not watched over me for good. Not that I had loft thofe ideas which chiefly engaged my heart to *England*, but defpair of feeing them accomplifhed, made me willing to remain where I was. I thought I could more eafily bear the difappointment in this fituation than nearer home. But, fo foon as I had fixed my connections and plans with thefe views, the Lord providentially interpofed to break them in pieces, and fave me from ruin in fpite of myfelf.

In the mean time, the fhip that had orders to bring me home arrived at *Sierra Leon*: the Captain made inquiry for me there and at the *Bonanas*; but underftanding that I was at a great diftance in the country he thought no more about me. Without doubt the hand of God directed

my

my being placed at *Kittam* juſt at this time; for, as the ſhip came no nearer than the *Bonanas*, and ſtaid but a few days, if I had been at the *Plantanes* I could not perhaps have heard of her till ſhe had been ſailed. The ſame muſt have certainly been the event, had I been ſent to any other factory, of which my new maſter had ſeveral upon different rivers. But though the place I was at was a long way up a river, much more than a hundred miles diſtant from the *Plantanes*, yet, by the peculiar ſituation which I have already noticed, I was ſtill within a mile of the ſea coaſt. To make the interpoſition more remarkable, I was at that very juncture, going in queſt of trade to a place at ſome diſtance directly from the ſea, and ſhould have ſet out a day or two before, but that we waited for a few articles from the next ſhip that offered, to complete the aſſortment of goods I was to take with me. We uſed ſometimes to walk to the beach, in expectation of ſeeing a veſſel paſs by, but this was very precarious, as at that time the place was not at all reſorted to by ſhips for trade. Many paſſed in the night, others kept at a conſiderable diſtance from the ſhore. In a word,

word, I do not know that any one had stopped while I was there, though some had before, upon obseiving a signal made from the shore. In *February* 1747, (I know not the exact day) my fellow-servant walking down to the beach in the forenoon, saw a vessel sailing past; and made a smoke in token of trade. She was already a little beyond the place, and, as the wind was fair, the Captain was in some demur whether to stop or not: however, had my companion been half an hour later, she would have been gone beyond recall; but he soon saw her come to an anchor, and went on board in a canoe; and this proved the very ship I have spoken of. One of the first questions he was asked was concerning me; and when the Captain understood I was so near, he came on shore to deliver his message. Had an invitation from home reached me, when I was sick and starving at the *Plantanes*, I should have received it as life from the dead; but now, for the reasons already given, I heard it at first with indifference. The Captain, unwilling to lose me, told a story altogether of his own framing; he gave me a very plausible account, how he had missed a large packet of letters and

papers,

papers, which he fhould have brought with him; but this, he faid, he was fure of, having had it from my father's own mouth, as well as from his employer, that a perfon, lately dead, had left me £400 *per annum*, adding further, that if I was any ways embarraffed in my circumftances, he had exprefs orders to redeem me, though it fhould coft one half of his cargo. Every particular of this was falfe; nor could I myfelf believe what he faid about the eftate; but, as I had fome expectations from an aged relation, I thought a part of it might be true. But I was not long in fufpenfe: for though my father's care and defire to fee me had too little weight with me, and would have been infufficient to make me quit my retreat, yet the remembrance of Mrs. ———, the hopes of feeing her, and the poffibility, that accepting this offer might once more put me in a way of gaining her hand, prevailed over all other confiderations. The Captain further promifed (and in this he kept his word) that I fhould lodge in his cabin, dine at his table, and be his conftant companion, without expecting any fervice from me. And thus I was fuddenly freed from a captivity of about fifteen months.

months. I had neither a thought nor a
defire of this change one hour before it
took place. I embarked with him, and in
a few hours loft fight of *Kittam*.

How much is their blindnefs to be
pitied, who can fee nothing but chance in
events of this fort! So blind and ftupid
was I at that time, I made no reflection.
I fought no direction in what had happened: like a wave of the fea driven with the
wind, and toffed, I was governed by prefent appearances, and looked no farther.
But he, who is eyes to the blind, was
leading me in a way that I knew not.

Now I am in fome meafure enlightened,
I can eafily perceive that it is in the adjuft-
ment and concurrence of thefe feemingly
fortuitous circumftances, that the ruling
power and wifdom of God is moft evidently
difplayed in human affairs. How many
fuch cafual events may we remark in the
hiftory of *Jofeph*, which had each a neceffary influence in his enfuing promotion!
If he had not dreamed, or if he had not
told his dream,—if the *Midianites* had
paffed by a day fooner or a day later; if
they had fold him to any perfon but *Poti-
phar*; if his miftrefs had been a better
D 5 woman;

woman; if *Pharaoh*'s officers had not difpleafed their Lord; or if any, or all thefe
things had fell out in any other manner
or time than they did, all that followed had
been prevented; the promifes and purpofes of God concerning *Ifrael*, their bond-
age, deliverances, polity, and fettlement,
muft have failed; and, as all thefe things
tended to, and centered in *Chrift*, the promifed Saviour, the defire of all nations
would not have appeared; mankind had
been ftill in their fins, without hope, and
the counfels of God's eternal love in
favour of finners defeated. Thus we may
fee a connection between *Jofeph*'s firft
dream, and the death of our Lord Chrift,
with all its glorious confequences. So
ftrong, though fecret, is the concatenation
between the *greateft* and the *fmalleft* events!
What a comfortable thought is this to a
believer to know, that amidft all the various interfering defigns of men, the Lord
has one conftant defign which he cannot,
will not mifs, namely, his own glory in
the complete falvation of his people; and
that he is wife, and ftrong, and faithful,
to make even thofe things, which feem
contrary to this defign, fubfervient to
promote

promote it. You have allowed me to comment upon my own text, yet the length of this obſervation may need ſome apology. Believe me to be, with great reſpect,

Dear Sir,

Your affectionate and obliged ſervant.

January 18, 1763.

LETTER.

LETTER VII.

DEAR SIR,

THE ship I was now on board, as a passenger, was on a trading voyage for *gold, ivory, dyers' wood,* and *bees' wax.* It requires much longer time to collect a cargo of this sort than of slaves. The Captain began his trade at *Gambia,* had been already four or five months in *Africa,* and continued there a year, or thereabouts, after I was with him; in which time we ranged the whole coast, as far as *Cape Lopez,* which lies about a degree south of the Equinoctial, and more than a thousand miles farther from *England,* than the place where I embarked. I have little to offer worthy your notice, in the course of this tedious voyage. I had no business to employ my thoughts but sometimes amused myself with *mathematics:* excepting this, my whole life, when awake, was a course of most horrid impiety and profaneness. I know not that I

have

have ever since met so daring a blasphemer: not content with common oaths and imprecations, I daily invented new ones; so that I was often seriously reproved by the Captain, who was himself a very passionate man and not at all circumspect in his expressions. From the relation I at times made him of my past adventures, and what he saw of my conduct, and especially towards the close of the voyage when we met with many disasters, he would often tell me that, to his great grief, he had a *Jonah* on board; that a curse attended me wherever I went; and that all the troubles he met with in the voyage, were owing to his having taken me into the vessel. I shall omit any further particulars, and after mentioning an instance or two of the Lord's mercy to me, while I was thus defying his power and patience, I shall proceed to something more worthy your perusal.

Although I lived long in the excess of almost every other extravagance, I never was fond of drinking; and my father has often been heard to say, that while I avoided drunkenness, he should still entertain hopes of my recovery. But sometimes

‘ ꞓes I would promote a drinking-bout
      a frolic-fake, as I termed it; for
though I did not love the liquor, I was
fold to do iniquity, and delighted in mifchief. The laft abominable frolic of this
fort I engaged in, was in the river *Gabon*;
the propofal and expence were my own.
Four or five of us one evening fat down
upon deck, to fee who could hold out
longeft in drinking geneva and rum alternately; a large fea-fhell fupplied the
place of a glafs. I was very unfit for a
challenge of this fort, for my head was
always incapable of bearing much ftrong
drink. However, I began and propofed
the firft toaft, which, I well remember,
was fome imprecation againft the perfon
who fhould *ftart* firft.——This proved to
be myfelf.——My brain was foon fired:——
I arofe, and danced about the deck like
a madman; and while I was thus di-
verting my companions, my hat went
over-board. By the light of the moon I
faw the fhip's boat, and eagerly threw
myfelf over the fide to get into her, that I
might recover my hat. My fight in that
circumftance deceived me, for the boat
was not within my reach, as I had thought,
but perhaps twenty feet from the fhip's
                                    fide.

fide. I was, however, half over-board,
and fhould in one moment more have
plunged myfelf into the water, when
fomebody catched hold of my clothes
behind, and pulled me back. This was
an amazing efcape, for I could not fwim
if I had been fober; the tide ran very
ftrong, my companions were too much
intoxicated to fave me, and the reft of
the fhip's company were afleep. So near
I was, to appearance, of perifhing in that
dreadful condition, and finking into eternity under the weight of my own curfe!

Another time, at *Cape Lopez*, fome of
us had been in the woods, and fhot a
buffalo or *wild cow*, we brought a part
of it on board, and carefully marked the
place (as I thought) where we left the
remainder. In the evening we returned
to fetch it, but we fet out too late. I
undertook to be their guide, but night
coming on before we could reach the
place, we loft our way—Sometimes we
were in fwamps up to the middle in water,
and when we recovered dry land, we
could not tell whether we were walking
towards the fhip, or wandering farther
from her.—Every ftep increafed our uncertainty.—The night grew darker, and
we

we were entangled in inextricable woods,
where, perhaps, the foot of man had never
trod before. That part of the country is
entirely abandoned to wild beafts, with
which it prodigiously abounds. We were
indeed in a terrible cafe, having neither
light, food, or arms, and expecting a tiger
to rufh from behind every tree. The
ftars were clouded, and we had no com-
pafs to form a judgment which way we
were going. Had things continued thus,
we had probably perifhed: but it pleafed
God, no beaft came near us; and, after
fome hours perplexity, the moon arofe,
and pointed out the eaftern quarter. It
appeaied then, as we had expected, that
inftead of drawing near to the fea-fide,
we had been penetrating into the country;
but, by the guidance of the moon, we at
length came to the water-fide, a confiderable diftance from the fhip. We got
fafe on board, without any other inconve-
nience than what we fuffered from fear
and fatigue.

Thofe and many other deliverances,
were all, at that time entirely loft upon
me. The admonitions of confcience,
which, fiom fucceffive repulfes, had grown
weaker and weaker, at length entirely
ceafed;

ceafed; and for a fpace of many months,
if not for fome years, I cannot recollect,
that I had a fingle check of that fort.
At times I have been vifited with ficknefs, and have believed myfelf near to
death, but I had not the leaft concern
about the confequences. In a word, I
feemed to have every mark of final im-
penitence and rejection; neither judg-
ments nor mercies made the leaft impreffion on me.

At length, our bufinefs finifhed, we left
Cape Lopez, and after a few days ftay at
the ifland of *Annabona*, to lay in provifions, we failed homeward about the beginning of *January*, 1748. From *Annabona* to *England*, without touching at any
intermediate port, is a very long navigation, perhaps more than feven thoufand
miles, if we include the circuits neceffary to be made on account of the trade-
winds. We failed firft weftward, till
near the coaft of *Brazil*, then northward, to the banks of *Newfoundland*, with
the ufual variations of wind and weather, and without meeting any thing extraordinary. On thefe banks we ftopped
half a day to fifh for cod: this was then
chiefly for diverfion; we had provifions
enough,

enough, and little expected thofe fifh (as it afterwards proved) would be all we fhould have to fubfift on. We left the banks *March* firft, with a hard gale of wind wefterly, which pufhed us faft homewards. I fhould heie obferve, that with the length of this voyage in a hot climate, the veffel was greatly out of repair, and very unfit to fupport ftormy weather: the fails and cordage were likewife very much worn out, and many fuch circumftances concurred to render what followed more dangerous. I think it was on the ninth of *March*, the day before our cataftrophe, that I felt a thought pafs through my mind which I had long been a ftranger to. Among the few books we had on board, one was *Stanhope*'s *Thomas à Kempis*; I carelefsly took it up, as I had often done before, to pafs away the time; but I had ftill read it with the fame indifference as if it was entirely a romance. However, while I was reading this time, an involuntary fuggeftion arofe in my mind — what if thefe things fhould be true? I could not bear the force of the inference, as it related to myfelf, and therefore fhut the book prefently. My confcience witneffed againft me once more,

and

and I concluded that, true or falfe, I muft abide the confequences of my own choice. I put an abrupt end to thefe reflections, by joining in with fome vain converfation or other that came in my way.

But now the *Lord's time was come*, and the conviction I was fo unwilling to receive, was deeply impreffed upon me by an awful difpenfation. I went to bed that night in my ufual fecurity and indifference, but was awaked from a found fleep by the force of a violent fea which broke on board us; fo much of it came down below as filled the cabin I lay in with water. This alarm was followed by a cry from the deck, that the fhip was going down or finking. As foon as I could recover myfelf, I effayed to go upon deck, but was met upon the ladder by the Captain, who defired me to bring a knife with me. While I returned for the knife another perfon went up in my room, who was inftantly wafhed overboard. We had no leifure to lament him, nor did we expect to furvive him long; for we foon found the fhip was filling with water very faft. The fea had torn away the upper timbers on one fide, and made a mere wreck in a few minutes. I fhall not affect

fect to defcribe this difafter in the marine
dialect, which would be underftood by
few. and therefore I can give you but a
very inadequate idea of it. Taken in all
circumftances it was aftonifhing, and almoft miraculous, that any of us furvived
to relate the ftory. We had immediate
recourfe to the pumps, but the water increafed againft oui efforts: fome of us
were fet to *bailing* in another part of the
veffel, that is, to lade it out with buckets
and pails. We had but eleven or twelve
people to fuftain this fervice; and, notwithftanding all we could do, fhe was full,
or very near it; and then with a common
cargo, fhe muft have funk of courfe: but
we had a great quantity of bees wax and
wood on board, which were fpecifically
lighter than the water; and as it pleafed
God, that we received this fhock in the
very crifis of the gale, towards morning
we were enabled to employ fome means
for our fafety, which fucceeded beyond
hope. In about an hour's time the day
began to break, and the wind abated.
We expended moft of our clothes and
bedding to ftop the leaks (though the
weather was exceeding cold, efpecially to
us who had fo lately left a hot climate)

over

over thefe we nailed pieces of boards, and at laft perceived the water abate. At the beginning of this hurry, I was little affected; I pumped hard, and endeavoured to animate myfelf and my companions: I told one of them that in a few days this diftrefs would ferve us to talk of over a glafs of wine; but he being a lefs hardened finner than myfelf, replied with tears, "No, it is too late now." About nine o'clock, being almoft fpent with cold and labour, I went to fpeak with the Captain, who was bufied elfewhere, and juft as I was returning from him, I faid, almoft without any meaning, "If this will not do the Lord have mercy upon us." This (though fpoken with little reflection) was the firft defire I had breathed for mercy for the fpace of many years. I was inftantly ftruck with my own words, and as *Jehu* faid once, *What haft thou to do with peace?* fo it directly occurred, *What mercy can there be for me?* I was obliged to return to the pump, and there I continued till noon, almoft every paffing wave breaking over my head; but we made ourfelves faft with ropes, that we might not be wafhed away. Indeed I expected that every time the veffel defcended in the

fea,

sea, she would rise no more; and though I dreaded death *now*, and my heart foreboded the worst, if the scriptures which I had long since opposed, were indeed true; yet still I was but half convinced, and remained for a space of time in a sullen frame, a mixture of despair and impatience. I thought, if the christian religion was true I could not be forgiven; and was therefore expecting, and almost, at times, wishing to know the worst of it.

I am,

Your's, &c.

January 17, 1763.

LETTER VIII.

DEAR SIR,

THE tenth (that is in the prefent ftyle the twenty-firft) of *March*, is a day much to be remembered by me, and I have never fuffered it to pafs wholly unnoticed fince the year 1748. On that day the Lord fent from on high, and delivered me out of the deep waters.—I continued at the pump from *three* in the *morning* till near *noon*, and then I could do no more: I went and lay down upon my bed, un-certain and almoft indifferent whether I fhould rife again. In an hour's time I was called, and not being able to pump, I went to the elm and fteered the fhip till midnight, excepting a fmall interval for refrefhment. I had here leifure and convenient opportunity for reflection: I began to think of my former religious pro-feffions, the extraordinary turns in my life; the calls, warnings, and deliverances I had met with, the licentious courfe of my converfation, particularly my unparalleled

effrontery

effrontery in making the gofpel hiftory
(which I could not now be fure was falfe,
though I was not yet affured it was true)
the conftant fubject of profane ridicule. I
thought, allowing the fcripture premifes,
there never was nor could be fuch a finner
as myfelf, and then comparing the advantages I had broken through, I concluded,
at firft, that my fins were too great to be
forgiven. The fcripture likewife feemed
to fay the fame; for I had formerly been
well acquainted with the Bible, and many
paffages, upon this occafion, returned
upon my memory, particularly thofe awful
paffages *Prov.* i. 24—31. *Heb.* vi. 4, 6.
and 2 *Pet.* ii. 20. which feemed fo exactly to fuit my cafe and character, as to
bring with them a prefumptive proof of a
divine original. Thus, as I have faid,
I waited with fear and impatience to receive my inevitable doom. Yet, though
I had thoughts of this kind, they were
exceeding faint and difproportionate; it
was not till long after (perhaps feveral
years) till I had gained fome clear views
of the infinite righteoufnefs and grace of
Chrift Jefus my Lord, that I had a deep
and ftrong apprehenfion of my ftate by
nature and practice, and perhaps, till then
I could .

I could not have borne the fight. So wonderfully does the Lord proportion the discoveries of sin and grace; for he knows our frame, and that if he was to put forth the greatness of his power, a poor sinner would be instantly overwhelmed, and crushed as a moth. But to return; when I saw, beyond all probability, there was still hope of respite, and heard about six in the evening that the ship was freed from water, there arose a gleam of hope. I thought I saw the hand of God displayed in our favour, I began to pray; I could not utter the prayer of faith, I could not draw near to a reconciled God and call him father: my prayer was like the cry of the ravens, which yet the Lord does not disdain to hear. I now began to think of that *Jesus* whom I had so often derided; I recollected the particulars of his life and of his death; a death for sins not his *own*, but, as I remembered, for the sake of those who, in their distress, should put their trust in him. And now I chiefly wanted evidence.——The comfortless principles of infidelity were deeply riveted, and I rather wished than believed these things were real facts. You will please to observe, Sir, that I collect the

E ftrain

ftrain of the reafonings and exercifes of my mind in one view; but I do not fay that all this paffed at one time. The great queftion now was, how to obtain *faith?* I fpeak not of an appropriating faith (of which I then knew neither the nature nor neceffity) but how I fhould gain an affurance that the fcriptures were of a divine infpiration, and a fufficient warrant for the exercife of truft and hope in God. One of the firft helps I received (in confequence of a determination to examine the New Teftament more carefully) was from *Luke* xi. 13. I had been fenfible, that to profefs faith in Jefus Chrift, when, in reality, I did not believe his hiftory, was no better than a mockery of the heart-fearching God; but here I found a fpirit fpoken of which was to be communicated to thofe who afk it. Upon this I reafoned thus: if this book is true, the promife in this paffage muft be true likewife: I have need of that very fpirit, by which the whole was wrote, in order to underftand it aright. He has engaged here to give that fpirit to thofe who afk. I muft therefore pray for it, and, if it is of God, he will make good his own word. My purpofes were ftrengthened by *John* vii. 17.

17. I concluded from thence, that though I could not fay from my heart, that I be-lieved the gofpel, yet I would, for the prefent, take it for granted; and that, by ftudying it in this light, I fhould be more and more confirmed in it. If what I am writing could be perufed by our modern infidels, they would fay (for I too well know their manner) that I was very defirous to perfuade myfelf into this opinion. I confefs I was, and fo would they be, if the Lord fhould fhew them, as he was pleafed to fhew me at that time, the abfolute neceffity of fome expedient to interpofe between a righteous God and a finful foul; upon the gofpel fcheme I faw, at leaft, a peradventure of hope, but on every other fide I was furrounded with black unfathomable defpair.

The wind was now moderate, but continued fair, and we were ftill drawing nearer to our port. We began to recover from our confternation, though we were greatly alarmed by our circumftances. We found that the water, having floated all our moveables in the hold, all the cafks of provifion had been beaten to pieces by the violent motion of the fhip: on the other hand, our live ftock, fuch as

pigs,

pigs, sheep and poultry, had been washed over-board in the storm. In effect, all the provisions we saved, except the fish I had mentioned, and some food of the pulse kind, which used to be given to the hogs, (and there was but little of this left) all our other provisions would have subsisted us but a week at scanty allowance. The sails too were mostly blown away, so that we advanced but slowly, even while the wind was fair. We imagined ourselves about a hundred leagues from the land, but were in reality much farther. Thus we proceeded with an alternate prevalence of hope and fear.— My leisure time was chiefly employed in reading and meditating on the scripture, and praying to the Lord for mercy and instruction.

Things continued thus for four or five days, or perhaps longer, till we were awakened one morning by the joyful shouts of the watch upon deck, proclaiming the sight of land. We were all soon raised at the sound. The dawning was uncommonly beautiful, and the light (just strong enough to discover distant objects) presented us with a gladdening prospect: it seemed a mountainous coast, about twenty miles from us, terminating in a

cape

cape or point, and a little farther two
or three fmall iflands, or hammocks, as if
juft rifing out of the water; the appearance and pofition feemed exactly anfwer-
able to our hopes, refembling the north
weft extremity of *Ireland*, which we were
fteering for. We fincerely congratulated
each other, making no doubt, but that if
the wind continued we fhould be in fafety
and plenty the next day. The fmall remainder of our brandy (which was reduced
to little more than a pint) was, by the Captain's orders diftributed amongft us; he
adding at the fame time, " We fhall foon
have brandy enough." We likewife eat
up the refidue of our bread, for joy of
this welcome fight, and were in the condition of men fuddenly reprieved from
death. While we were thus alert, the
mate with a graver tone than the reft,
funk our fpirits by faying, that " he
wifhed it might prove land at laft." If
one of the common failors had firft faid fo,
I know not but the reft would have beat
him for raifing fuch an unreafonable doubt.
It brought on, however, warm debates and
difputes whether it was land or no; but
the cafe was foon unanfwerably decided,
for the day was advancing faft, and in a

little

little time, one of our fancied iflands began to grow red, from the approach of the
fun which foon arofe juft under it. In a
word, we had been prodigal of our bread
and brandy too haftily; our land was
literally *in nubibus*, nothing but clouds,
and in half an hour more the whole appearance was diffipated. — Sea-men have
often known deceptions of this fort, but
in our extremity we were very loath to be
undeceived. However, we comforted ourfelves that though we could not fee the
land, yet we fhould foon, the wind hitherto
continuing fair; but alas, we were deprived of this hope likewife! — That very
day our fair wind fubfided into a calm,
and the next morning the gales fprung
up from the fouth eaft, directly againft
us, and continued fo for more than a
fortnight afterwards. The fhip was fo
wrecked, that we were obliged to keep
the wind always on the broken fide,
unlefs the whether was quite moderate:
thus we were driven by the wind fixing
in that quarter, ftill further from our port,
to the northward of all *Ireland*, as far as
the *Lewis* or weftern iflands of *Scotland*,
but a long way to the weftward. In a word,
our ftation was fuch, as deprived us of
any

any hope of being relieved by other veffels : it may indeed be queftioned whether our fhip was not in the very fiift that had been in that part of the ocean, at the fame feafon of the year.

Provifions now began to grow very fhort; the half of a falted cod was a day's fubfiftence for twelve people; we had plenty of frefh water, but not a drop of ftronger liquor ; no bread, hardly any clothes, and very cold weather. We had inceffant labour with the pumps, to keep the fhip above water. Much labour and little food wafted us faft, and one man died under the hardfhip. Yet our fufferings were light in comparifon of our juft fears; we could not afford this bare allowance much longer, but had a terrible piofpect of being either ftarved to death, or reduced to feed upon one another. Our expectations grew darker eveiy day, and I had a further trouble peculiar to myfelf. The Captain, whofe tempei was quite fouied by diftiefs, was hourly reproaching me (as I formerly obferved) as the fole caufe of the calamity, and was confident that if I was thrown over-board (and not otherwife) they fhould be preferved from death. He did not intend to make the

experiment,

experiment, but the continual repetition of this in my ears gave me much uneafinefs, efpecially as my confcience feconded his words, I thought it very probable that all that had befallen us was on my account. I was, at laft, found out by the powerful hand of God and condemned in my own breaft. However, proceeding in the method I have defcribed, we began to conceive hopes greater than all our fears, efpecially when at the time we were ready to give up all for loft, and defpair was taking place in every countenance, we faw the wind come about to the very point we wifhed it, fo as beft to fuit that broken part of the fhip which muft be kept out of the water, and to blow fo gentle as our few remaining fails could bear, and thus it continued without any obfervable alteration or increafe, though at an unfettled time of the year, till we once more were called up to fee the land, and were convinced that it was land indeed. We faw the ifland *Tory*, and the next day anchored in *Lough Swilly* in *Ireland*, this was the eighth of *April*, juft four weeks after the damage we fuftained from the fea. When we came into this port our very laft victuals were boiling in the pot, and
                                        before

before we had been there two hours, the wind, which feemed to have been providentially reftrained till we were in a place of fafety, began to blow with great violence, fo that if we had continued at fea that night in our fhattered enfeebled condition, we muft in all human appearance, have gone to the bottom. About this time I began to know that there is a God that hears and anfwers prayer. How many times has he appeared for me fince this great deliverance:—yet, alas! how diftruftful and ungrateful is my heart unto this hour.

I am, dear SIR,

Your obliged humble fervant.

JANUARY 18, 1763.

LETTER

LETTER IX.

DEAR SIR,

I HAVE brought my hiſtory down to the time of my arrival in *Ireland* 1748; but before I proceed I would look back a little, to give you ſome farther account of the ſtate of my mind, and how far I was helped againſt inward difficulties, which beſet me, at the time I had many outward hardſhips to ſtruggle with. The ſtraits of hunger, cold, wearineſs, and the fears of ſinking and ſtarving, I ſhared in common with others, but beſides theſe, I felt a heart-bitterneſs, which was properly my own; no one on board but myſelf being impreſſed with any ſenſe of the hand of God in our danger and deliverance, at leaſt not awakened to any concern for their ſouls. No temporal diſpenſations can reach the heart, unleſs the Lord himſelf applies them. My companions in danger were either quite unaffected, or ſoon forgot it all, but it was not ſo with me: not that I was any wiſer or

better

better than they, but becaufe the Lord
was pleafed to vouchfafe me peculiar mercy, otherwife I was the moft unlikely perfon in the fhip to receive an impreffion,
having been often before quite ftupid and
hardened in the very face of great dangers,
and always to this time had hardened
my neck ftill more and more after every
reproof.—I can fee no reafon, why the
Lord fingled me out for mercy but this,
" that fo it feemed good to him;" ùn-
lefs it was to fhew, by one aftonifhing inftance, that with him " nothing is impoffible."

Theie were no perfons on board, to
whom I could open myfelf with freedom
concerning the ftate of my fóul, none
fiom whom I could afk advice. As to
books, I had a *New Teftament*, *Stanhope*
already mentioned, and a volume of
Bifhop *Beveridge*'s fermons, one of which
upon our Lord's paffion affected me much.
In perufing the *New Teftament*, I was
ftiuck with feveial paffages, particularly
that of the fig-tree, *Luke* xiii. The cafe
of St. *Paul*, 1 *Tim.* i. but particularly the
Prodigal, *Luke* xv. a cafe I thought that
had never been fo nearly exemplified, a
by myfelf—and then the goodnefs of the

E 6

father

father in receiving, nay, in running to meet such a son, and this intended only to illustrate the Lord's goodness to returning sinners—this gained upon me: I continued much in prayer: I saw that the Lord had interposed *so far* to save me, and I hoped he would do more. The outward circumstances helped in this place, to make me still more serious and earnest in crying to him, who alone could relieve me; and sometimes I thought I could be content to die even for want of food, so I might but die a believer. Thus far I was answered, that before we arrived in *Ireland* I had a satisfactory evidence in my own mind of the truth of the gospel, as considered in itself, and its exact suitableness to answer all my needs. I saw that, by the way they were pointed out, God might declare not his mercy only, but his justice also, in the pardon of sin, on the account of the obedience and sufferings of Jesus Christ. My judgment, at that time, embraced the sublime doctrine of " God manifest in the flesh, reconciling the world to himself." I had no idea of those systems, which allow the Saviour no higher honour than that of an *upper servant,* or, at the most, a *demigod.*

I stood

I stood in need of an Almighty Saviour, and such a one I found described in the *New Testament*. Thus far the Lord had wrought a marvellous thing; I was no longer an infidel; I heartily renounced my former profaneness, and I had taken up some right notions, was seriously disposed, and sincerely touched with a sense of the undeserved mercy I had received, in being brought safe through so many dangers. I was sorry for my past mis-spent life, and purposed an immediate reformation: I was quite freed from the habit of swearing, which seemed to have been deeply rooted in me, as a second nature. Thus to all appearance I was a new man.

But though I cannot doubt that this change, so far as it prevailed, was wrought by the spirit and power of God, yet still I was greatly deficient in many respects. I was in some degree affected with a sense of my more enormous sins, but I was little aware of the innate evils of my heart. I had no apprehension of the spirituality and extent of the law of God: the hidden life of a christian, as it consists in communion with God by Jesus Christ, and a continual dependence on

him

him for hourly fupplies of wifdom,
ftrength, and comfort, was a myftery of
which I had as yet no knowledge. I ac-
knowledged the Lord's mercy in pardoning what was paft, but depended chiefly
upon my own refolution to do better for
the time to come. I had no chriftian
friend or faithful minifter to advife me,
that my ftrength was no more than my
righteoufnefs; and though I foon began
to inquire for ferious books, yet, not
having fpiritual difcernment, I frequently
made a wrong choice, and I was not
brought in the way of evangelical preaching or converfation (except the few times
when I heard but underftood not) for fix
years after this period. Thofe things the
Lord was pleafed to difcover to me
gradually. I learnt them here a little
and there a little, by my own painful
experience, at a diftance from the common means and ordinances, and in the
midft of the fame courfe of evil company and bad examples I had been converfant with for fome time. From this
period I could no more make a mock
at fin, or jeft with holy things; I no more
queftioned the truth of fcripture, or loft
a fenfe of the rebukes of confcience.
There-

Therefore I consider this as the beginning of my return to God, or rather of his return to me; but I cannot consider myself to have been a believer (in the full sense of the word) till a considerable time afterwards.

I have told you that, in the time of our distress, we had fresh water in abundance; this was a considerable relief to us, especially as our spare diet was mostly salt fish, without bread. We drank plentifully, and were not afraid of wanting water, yet our stock of this likewise was much nearer to an end than we expected: we supposed that we had six large butts of water on board, and it was well that we were safe arrived in *Ireland* before we discovered that five of them were empty, having been removed out of their places and stove by the violent agitation, when the ship was full of water. If we had found this out while we were at sea, it would have greatly heightened our distress, as we must have drank more sparingly.

While the ship was refitting at *Lough Swilly*, I repaired to *Londonderry*. I lodged at an exceeding good house, where I was treated with much kindness, and soon

recruited

recruited my health and ftrength. I was
now a ferious profeffor, went twice a day
to the prayers at church, and determined
to receive the facrament the next opportunity. A few days before I fignified
my intention to the minifter, as the rubric
directs ; but I found this practice was
grown obfolete. At length the day came:
I arofe very early, was very particular
and earneft in my private devotion, and,
with the greateft folemnity, engaged myfelf to be the Lord's for ever, and only
his. This was not a formal, but a fincere
furrender, under a warm fenfe of mercies
recently received; and yet, for want of a
better knowledge of myfelf and the
fubtilty of Satan's temptations, I was feduced to forget the vows of God that
were upon me. Upon the whole, though
my views of the gofpel falvation were
very indiftinct, I experienced a peace and
fatisfaction in the ordinance that day,
to which I had been hitherto a perfect
ftranger.

The next day I was abroad with the
Mayor of the city and fome other gen-
tlemen a fhooting ; I climbed up a fteep
bank, and pulling my fowling-piece after
me

me, as I held it in a perpendicular direction, it went off fo near my face as to
burn away the corner of my hat. Thus,
when we think ourfelves in the greateft
fafety, we are no lefs expofed to danger
than when all the elements feem con-
fpiring to deftroy us. The Divine Providence, which is fufficient to deliver us
in our utmoft extremity, is equally neceffary to our prefervation in the moft
peaceful fituation.

During our ftay in *Ireland* I wrote
home. The veffel I was in had not been
heard of for eighteen months, and was
given up for loft long before. My father
had no more expectation of hearing that
I was alive, but he received my letter a
few days before he left *London.*—He was
juft going Governor of *York Fort,* in *Hud-
fon's Bay,* from whence he never returned.
He failed before I landed in *England,* or
he had purpofed to take me with him;
but God defigning otherwife, one hindrance or other delayed us in *Ireland* till
it was too late. I received two or three
affectionate letters from him, but I never
had the pleafure of feeing him more. I
had hopes, that in three years more I
fhould have had an opportunity of afking
his

his forgivenefs for the uneafinefs my difobedience had given him; but the fhip,
that was to have brought him home,
came without him. According to the
beft accounts we received, he was feized
with the cramp, when bathing, and
drowned a little before her arrival in the
Bay.—Excufe this digreffion.

My father, willing to contribute all in
his power to my fatisfaction, paid a vifit
before his departure to my friends in
Kent, and gave his confent to the union
which had been fo long talked of. Thus,
when I returned to ————, I found I
had only the confent of one perfon to
obtain: with her I as yet ftood at as
great an uncertainty as on the firft day I
faw her.

I arrived at ———— the latter end of
May 1748, about the fame day that my
father failed from the *Nore,* but found
the Lord had provided me another father
in the gentleman whofe fhip had brought
me home. He received me with great
tendernefs, and the ftrongeft expreffions
of friendfhip and affiftance, yet not more
than he has fince made good: for to him,
as the inftrument of God's goodnefs, I
owe my all. Yet it would not have been

in

in the power even of this friend, to have
ferved me effectually, if the Lord had not
met with me on my way home, as I have
·related. Till then I was like the man
poffeffed with the *legion*. No arguments,
no perfuafion, no views of intereft, no
remembrance of the paft, or regard to
the future, could have conftrained me
within the bounds of common prudence.
But now I was in fome meafure reftored
to my fenfes. My friend immediately
offered me the command of a fhip; which,
upon mature confideration, I declined
for the prefent. I had been hitherto always unfettled and carelefs, and therefore
thought I had better make another voyage
firft, and learn to obey and acquire a
farther infight and experience in bufinefs,
before I ventured to undertake fuch a
charge. The mate of the veffel I came
home in, was preferred to the command
of a new fhip, and I engaged to go in
the ftation of mate with him. I made a
fhort vifit to *London*, &c. which did not
fully anfwer my views. I had but one
opportunity of feeing Mrs. ******, of
which I availed myfelf very little, for I
was always exceeding awkward in plead-
ing my own caufe, *viva voce.*—But after
my

my return to L————, I put the queftion in fuch a manner, by letter, that fhe could not avoid (unlefs I had greatly miftaken her) coming to fome fort of an explanation. Her anfwer (though penned with abundance of caution) fatisfied me, as I collected from it, that fhe was free from any other engagement, and not unwilling to wait the event of the voyage I had undertaken. I fhould be afhamed to trouble you with thefe little details, if you had not yourfelf defired me.

I am,

Your's &c.

LETTER

LETTER X.

DEAR SIR,

MY connections with sea affairs have often led me to think, that the varieties observable in christian experience may be properly illustrated from the circumstances of a voyage. Imagine to yourself a number of vessels, at different times, and from different places, bound to the same port; there are some things in which all these would agree,—the compass steered by the port in view, the general rules of navigation, both as to the management of the vessel and determining their astronomical observation, would be the same in all. In other respects they would differ: perhaps no two of them would meet with the same distribution of winds and weather. Some we see set out with a prosperous gale, and, when they almost think their passage secured, they are checked by adverse blasts; and, after enduring much hardship and danger,

and

and frequent expectations of shipwreck, they just escape and reach the desired haven: others meet the greatest difficulties at first, they put forth in a storm, and are often beaten back; at length their voyage proves favourable, and they enter the port with a πληροφορια, a rich and abundant entrance. Some are hard beset with cruizers and enemies, and obliged to fight their way through; others meet with little remarkable in their passage. Is it not thus in the spiritual life? All true believers walk by the same rule, and mind the same things. The word of God is their compass, *Jesus* is both their polar star, and their sun of righteousness; their hearts and faces are all set *Sion* ward. Thus far they are as one body, animated by one spirit, yet their experience, formed upon these common principles, is far from uniform: the Lord in his first call, and his following dispensations, has a regard to the situation, temper, talents of each, and to the particular services or trials he has appointed them for. Though all are exercised at times, yet some pass through the voyage of life much more smoothly than others. But he, " who walks upon the
" wings

" wings of the wind, and meafures the
" waters in the hollow of his hand," will
not fuffer any, of whom he has once taken
charge, to perifh in the ftorms, though,
for a feafon, perhaps, many of them are
ready to give up all hopes.

We muft not, therefore, make the experience of others, in all refpects, a rule
to ourfelves, nor our own a rule to others:
yet thefe are common miftakes, and pro-
ductive of many more. As to myfelf,
every part of my cafe has been extraordinary—I have hardly met a fingle inftance
refembling it. Few, very few, have been
recovered from fuch a dreadful ftate : and
the few that have been thus favoured,
have generally paffed through the moft
fevere convictions, and, after the Lord
has given them peace, their future lives
have been ufually more zealous, bright,
and exemplary than common Now, as
on the one hand, my convictions were
very moderate, and far below what might
have been expected from the dreadful re-
view I had to make; fo, on the other, my
firft beginnings in a religious courfe were
as faint as can be well imagined. I never
knew that feafon alluded to, *Jer.* ii. 2.
Rev. ii. 4. ufually called the time of the

firft

firſt love. Who would not expect to
hear that, after ſuch a wonderful un-
hoped for deliverance as I had received,
and, after my eyes were in ſome meaſure
enlightened to ſee things aright, I ſhould
immediately cleave to the Lord and his
ways with full purpoſe of heart, and
conſult no more with fleſh and blood?
But, alas! it was far otherwiſe with me; I
had learned to pray, I ſet ſome value upon
the word of God, and was no longer a
libertine, but my ſoul ſtill cleaved to the
duſt. Soon after my departure from
L———, I began to intermit, and grow
ſlack in waiting upon the Lord: I grew
vain and trifling in my converſation; and
though my heart ſmote me often, yet my
armour was gone, and I declined faſt:
and by the time we arrived at *Guinea*, I
ſeemed to have forgotten all the Lord's
mercies and my own engagements, and
was (profaneneſs excepted) almoſt as bad
as before. The enemy prepared a train of
temptations, and I became his eaſy prey,
and for about a month he lulled me
aſleep in a courſe of evil, of which, a few
months before, I could not have ſuppoſed
myſelf any longer capable. How much
propriety is there in the apoſtle's advice,
"Take

" Take heed left any of you be hardened through the deceitfulnefs of fin." O who can be fufficiently upon their guard! Sin firft deceives, and then it hardens; I was now faft bound in chains; I had little defire, and no power at all to recover myfelf. I could not but at times reflect how it was with me; but, if I attempted to ftruggle with it, it was in vain. I was juft like *Samfon*, when he faid, " I will go forth and fhake myfelf as at other times," but the Lord was departed, and he found himfelf helplefs, in the hands of his enemies. By the remembrance of this interval, the Lord has often inftructed me fince, what a poor creature I am in myfelf, incapable of ftanding a fingle hour, without continual frefh fupplies of ftrength and grace from the fountain-head.

At length, the Lord, whofe mercies are infinite, interpofed in my behalf. My bufinefs, in this voyage, while upon the coaft, was to fail from place to place in the long-boat, to purchafe flaves. The fhip was at *Sierra Leon*, and I then at the *Plantanes*, the fcene of my former captivity, where every thing I faw might feem to remind me of my ingratitude. I

F

was

was in eafy circumftances, courted by
thofe who formerly defpifed me. The
lime trees I had planted were growing tall,
and promifed fruit the following year,
againft which time I had expectations of
returning with a fhip of my own. But
none of thefe things affected me, till, as I
have faid, the Lord again interpofed to
fave me. He vifited me with a violent
fever, which broke the fatal chain, and
once more brought me to myfelf. But oh,
what a profpect! I thought myfelf now
fummoned away—My paft dangers and
deliverances, my earneft prayers in the
time of trouble, my folemn vows before
the Lord at his table, and my ungrateful
returns for all his goodnefs, were all prefent to my mind at once. Then I began
to wifh that the Lord had fuffered me to
fink into the ocean, when I firft befought
his mercy. For a little while, I concluded
the door of hope to be quite fhut; but
this continued not long. Weak, and
almoft delirious, I arofe from my bed, and
crept to a retired part of the ifland; and
here I found a renewed liberty to pray.
I durft make no more refolves, but caft
myfelf before the Lord, to do with me as
he fhould pleafe. I do not remember,
that

that any particular text or remarkable difcovery was piefented to my mind; but in geneial I was enabled to hope and believe in a crucified Saviour. The burden was removed from my confcience, and not only my peace, but my health was reftored; I cannot fay inftantaneoufly, but I recovered from that hour, and fo faft, that when I returned to the fhip, two days afterwards, I was perfectly well before I got on board. And from that time, I truft, I have been delivered from the power and dominion of fin; though, as to the effects and conflicts of fin dwelling in me, I ftill " groan, being burdened." I now began again to wait upon the Lord, and though I have often grieved his fpirit, and foolifhly wandered from him fince (when, alas, fhall I be more wife!) yet his powerful grace has hitheito preferved me from fuch black declenfions as this I have laft recorded; and I humbly truft in his mercy and promifes, that he will be my guide and guard to the end.

My leifure hours in this voyage were chiefly employed in learning the *Latin* language, which I had now entirely forgot. This defire took place fiom an imi-

tation

tation I had seen of one of *Horace*'s Odes
in a magazine. I began the attempt under the greatest disadvantages possible;
for I pitched upon a poet, perhaps the
most difficult of the poets, even *Horace*
himself, for my first book. I had picked
up an old *English* translation of him,
which, with *Castalio's Latin* Bible, were
all my helps. I forgot a *Dictionary*, but
I would not therefore give up my purpose. I had the edition *in usum Delphini*,
and by comparing the Odes with the in-
terpretation, and tracing the words, I
could understand from one place to another, by the index, with the assistance I
could get from the *Latin* Bible: in this
way by dint of hard industry, often
waking when I might have slept, I made
some progress before I returned, and not
only understood the sense and meaning
of many Odes, and some of the Epistles,
but began to relish the beauties of the
composition, and acquired a spice of what
Mr. *Law* calls *classical enthusiasm*. And,
indeed, by this means I had *Horace* more
ad unguem than some who are masters of
the *Latin* tongue: for my helps were so
few that I generally had the passage fixed

in my memory, before I could fully understand its meaning.

My business in the long-boat, during eight months we were upon the coast, exposed me to innumerable dangers and perils, from burning suns, and chilling dews, winds, rains, and thunder-storms, in the open boat; and on shore, from long journeys through the woods and the temper of the natives, who are, in many places cruel, treacherous, and watching opportunities for mischief. Several boats in the same time were cut off; several white men poisoned, and, in my own boat, I buried six or seven people with fevers. When going on shore, or returning from it, in their little canoes, I have been more than once or twice overset, by the violence of the surf, or beach of the sea, and brought to land half dead, (for I could not swim). An account of such escapes, as I still remember, would swell to several sheets, and many more I have perhaps forgot; I shall only select one instance, as a specimen of that wonderful providence, which watched over me for good, and which, I doubt not, you will think worthy of notice.

F 3   When

When our trade was finifhed, and we were near failing to the *Weft Indies*, the only remaining fervice I had to perform in the boat, was to affift in bringing the wood and water from the fhore. We were then at *Rio Ceftors*. I ufed to go into the river in the afternoon, with the fea breeze, procure my loading in the evening, and return on board in the morning with the land-wind. Several of thefe little voyages I had made, but the boat was grown old, and almoft unfit for ufe. This fervice, likewife, was almoft completed. One day, having dined on board, I was preparing to return to the river, as formerly; I had taken leave of the Captain, received his - orders, was ready in the boat, and juft going to put off, as we term it, that is, to let go our ropes, and fail from the fhip. In that inftant, the Captain came up from the cabin, and called me on board again —I went, expecting further orders; but he faid he had *took it in his head* (as he phrafed it) that I fhould remain that day in the fhip, and accordingly ordered another man to go in my room. I was furprized at this, as the boat had never been fent away without me before; and

and afked him the reafon; he could give
me no reafon, but as above, that fo he
would have it. Accordingly, the boat
went without me, but returned no more.
She funk that night in the river, and
the perfon who had fupplied my place
was drowned. I was much ftruck when
we received news of the event the next
morning.—The Captain himfelf, though
quite a ftranger to religion, fo far as to
deny a particular providence, could not
help being affected; but he declared,
that he had no other reafon for coun-
termanding me at that time, but that
it came fuddenly into his mind to detain me.—I wonder I omitted this in
my eight letters, as I have always thought
it one of the moft extraordinary circumftances in my life.

I am, dear SIR,

Your humble fervant.

JANUARY 21, 1763.

LETTER

LETTER XI.

DEAR SIR,

A FEW days after I was thus wonderfully saved from an unforeseen danger,
we sailed for *Antigua*, and from thence
proceeded to *Charles-Town*, in *South
Carolina*. In this place there are many
serious people, but I knew not how to
find them out; indeed I was not aware
of a difference, but supposed that all
who attended public worship were good
christians. I was as much in the dark
about preaching, not doubting but what-
ever came from the pulpit must be very
good. I had two or three opportunities
of hearing a dissenting minister, named
Smith, who, by what I have known since,
I believe to have been an excellent and
powerful preacher of the gospel; and
there was something in his manner that
struck me, but I did not rightly understand him. The best words that men
can speak are ineffectual, till explained
and

and applied by the fpirit of God, who alone can open the heart. It pleafed the Lord for fome time, that I fhould learn no more than what he enabled me to collect from my own experience and reflection. My conduct was now very inconfiftent—almoft every day, when bufinefs would permit, I ufed to retire into the woods and fields (for thefe when at hand have always been my favourite oratories) and, I truft, I began to tafte the fweets of communion with God in the exercifes of prayer and praife, and yet I frequently fpent the evening in vain and worthlefs company; indeed, my relifh for worldly diverfions was much weakened, and I was rather a fpectatoi than a fharer in their pleafures, but I did not as yet fee the neceffity of an abfolute forbearance. Yet, as my compliance with cuftom and company was chiefly owing to want of light iather than to an obftinate attachment, and the Lord was pleafed to preferve me from what I *knew* was finful, I had, for the moft part, peace of confcience, and my ftrongeft defires were towards the things of God. As yet I knew not the force of that precept, " abftain from all appearance of evil," but

very

very often ventured upon the brink of
temptation; but the Lord was gracious
to my weakness, and would not suffer
the enemy to prevail against me. I did
not break with the world at once (as
might in my case - have been expected)
but I was gradually led to see the incon-
venience and folly of one thing after another, and, when I saw it, the Lord strength-
ened me to give it up. But it was some
years before I was set quite at liberty
from occasional compliances in many
things in which, at this time, I durst by
no means allow myself.

We finished our voyage, and arrived
in L————. When the ship's affairs
were settled I went to *London*, and from
thence (as you may suppose) I soon repaired to *Kent*. More than seven years
were now elapsed since my first visit. No
views of the kind could seem more chi-
merical, or could subsist under greater
discouragements than mine had done,
yet, through the over-ruling goodness of
God, while I seemed abandoned to myself, and blindly following my own head-
strong passions, I was guided by a hand
that I knew not, to the accomplishment
of my wishes. Every obstacle was now
removed:

removed: I had renounced my former follies, my interest was established, and friends on all sides consenting; the point was now entirely between ourselves, and after what had past, was easily concluded. ——Accordingly, our hands were joined on the first of *February* 1750.

The satisfaction I have found in this union, you will suppose has been greatly heightened, by reflection on the former disagreeable contrasts I had passed through, and the views I have had of the singular mercy and providence of the Lord · in bringing it to pass. If you please to look back to the beginning of my sixth letter, (page 84) I doubt not but you will allow, that few persons have known more, either of the misery or happiness, of which human life (as considered in itself) is capable. How easily, at a time of life when I was so little capable of judging, (but a few months more than seventeen) might my affections have been fixed where they could have met with no return, or where success would have been the heaviest disappointment. The long delay I met with was likewise a mercy; for had I succeeded a year or two sooner, before the Lord was pleased to change my heart,

F 6   we

we muft have been mutually unhappy, even as to the prefent life. " Surely " mercy and goodnefs have followed me " all my days."

But, alas! I foon began to feel that my heart was ftill hard and ungrateful to the God of my life. This crowning mercy, which raifed me to all I could afk or wifh in a temporal view, and which ought to have been an animating motive to obedi-ence and praife had a contrary effect.— I refted in the gift and forgot the giver. My poor narrow heart was *fatisfied*—A cold and carelefs frame, as to fpiritual things, took place and gained ground daily. Happy for me the feafon was advancing, and in *June* I received orders to repair to *L———*. This roufed me from my dream; I need not tell you, that I found the pains of abfence and fepa-ration fully proportioned to my preceding pleafure. It was hard, very hard, to part, efpecially as confcience interfered, and fuggefted to me how little I deferved that we fhould be fpared to meet again— But the Lord fupported me—I was a poor faint idolatrous creature, but I had now fome acquaintance with the way of accefs to a throne of grace, by the

the blood of Jesus, and peace was soon
restored to my conscience. Yet; through
all the following voyage, my irregular and
excessive affections were as thorns in my
eyes, and often made my other blessings
tasteless and insipid. But he who doth
all things well, over-ruled this likewise
for good. It became an occasion of quick-
ening me in prayer, both for her and myself; it increased my indifference for company and amusement; it habituated me
to a kind of voluntary self-denial, which
I was afterwards taught to improve to a
better purpose.

While I remained in *England,* we cor-
responded every post; and all the while
I used the sea afterwards, I constantly
kept up the practice of writing two or
three times a week (if weather and business permitted) though no conveyance
homeward offered for six or eight months
together. My packets were usually heavy,
and as not one of them at any time mis-
carried, I have to the amount of near two
hundred sheets of paper now lying in my
bureau of that correspondence. I mention
this little relief I had contrived to soften the
intervals of absence, because it had a
good effect beyond my first intention. It
                                    habituated

habituated me to think and write upon a great variety of subjects, and I acquired, insensibly, a greater readiness of expressing myself, than I should have otherwise attained. As I gained more ground in religious knowledge, my letters became more serious, and, at times, I still find an advantage in looking them over, especially as they remind me of many providential incidents, and the state of my mind at different periods in these voyages, which would otherwise have escaped my memory.

I sailed from *L———* in *August* 1750, commander of a good ship. I have no very extraordinary events to recount from this period, and shall therefore contract my memoirs, lest I become tedious; yet I am willing to give you a brief sketch of my history down to 1755, the year of my settlement in my present situation. I had now the command and care of thirty persons, I endeavoured to treat them with humanity, and to set them a good example; I likewise established public worship, according to the liturgy, twice every Lord's day, officiating myself. Farther than this I did not proceed, while I continued in that employment.

Having

Having now much leisure, I prosecuted the study of the *Latin* with good success. I remembered a Dictionary this voyage, and procured two or three other books; but still it was my hap to choose the hardest.—I added *Juvenal* to *Horace,* and for prose authors I pitched upon *Livy, Cæsar,* and *Salluft.* You will easily conceive, Sir, that I had hard work to begin (where I should have left off) with *Horace* and *Livy.* I was not aware of the difference of style; I had heard *Livy* highly commended, and was resolved to understand him. I began with the first page, and laid down a rule, which I seldom departed from, not to proceed to a second period till I understood the first, and so on. I was often at a stand, but seldom discouraged; here and there I found a few lines quite obstinate, and was forced to break in upon my rule, and give them up, especially as my edition had only the text, without any notes to assist me. But there were not many such, for, before the close of that voyage, I could (with a few exceptions) read *Livy* from end to end, almost as readily as an *English* author. And I found in surmounting this difficulty, I had surmounted all in one. Other

prose

profe authors, when they came in my
way, coft me little trouble. In fhort, in
the fpace of two or three voyages I became tolerably acquainted with the beft
claffics (I put all I have to fay upon this
fubject together): I read *Terence*, *Virgil*, and
feveral pieces of *Cicero* and the modern
claffics, *Buchanan*, *Erafmus*, and *Cafimir*;
at length I conceived a defign of becom-
ing *Ciceronian* myfelf, and thought it
would be a fine thing indeed to write
pure and elegant *Latin*.—I made fome
effays towards it, but by this time the
Lord was pleafed to draw me nearer to
himfelf, and to give me a fuller view
of the " pearl of great price," the in-
eftimable treafure hid in the field of the
holy fcripture; and, for the fake of this
I was made willing to part with all my
newly acquired riches. I began to think
that life was too fhort (efpecially my
life) to admit of leifure for fuch elabo-
rate trifling. Neither poet nor hiftorian
could tell me a word of *Jefus*, and I
therefore applied myfelf to thofe who
could. The claffics were at firft reftrained
to one morning in the week, and at length
quite laid afide. I have not looked in
Livy thefe five years, and I fuppofe I
could

could not now well underftand him. Some paffages in *Horace* and *Virgil* I ftill admire, but they feldom come in my way. I prefer *Buchanan*'s pfalms to a whole fhelf of *Elzevirs*.——But thus much I have gained, and more than this I am not folicitous about, fo much of the *Latin* as enables me to read any ufeful or curious book that is publifhed in that language. About the fame time, and for the fame reafon that I quarrelled with *Livy*, I laid afide the *mathematics*.——I found they not only coft me much time, but engroffed my thoughts too far: my head was literally full of *fchemes*. I was weary of cold contemplative truths, which can neither warm nor amend the heart, but rather tend to aggrandize *felf*. I found no traces of this wifdom in the life of *Jefus*, or the writings of *Paul*. I do not regret that I have had fome opportunities of knowing the firft principles of thefe things, but I fee much caufe to praife the Lord that he inclined me to ftop in time, and, whilft I was " fpending my labours for that which is " not bread," was pleafed to fet before me " wine and milk without money, and with- " out price."

My

My first voyage was fourteen months, through various scenes of danger and difficulty, but nothing very remarkable, and as I intend to be more particular with regard to the second, I shall only say that I was preserved from every harm; and having seen many fall on my right hand and on my left, I was brought home in peace, and restored to where my thoughts had been often directed *November* 2, 1751.

I am,

Your's, &c.

JANUARY 22, 1763.

LETTER

LETTER XII.

DEAR SIR,

I ALMOST wish I could recall my last sheet, and retract my promise. I fear I have engaged too far, and shall prove a mere *egotist*. What have I more that can deserve your notice? However, it is some satisfaction that I am now writing to yourself only, and, I believe, you will have candour to excuse, what nothing but a sense of your kindness could extort from me.

Soon after the period where my last closes, that is, in the interval between my first and second voyage after my marriage, I began to keep a sort of diary, a practice which I have since found of great use. I had in this interval repeated proofs of the ingratitude and evil of my heart. A life of ease, in the midst of my friends, and the full satisfaction of my wishes, was not favourable to the progress of grace, and afforded cause of daily humiliation. Yet, upon the whole, I gained ground. I

became

became acquainted with books, which
gave me a farther view of Chriftian doctrine and experience, particularly *Scougal's
Life of God in the Soul of Man*, *Hervey's
Meditations*, and *the Life of Colonel Gardner*.
As to preaching, I heard none, but of
the common fort, and had hardly an
idea of any better; neither had I the
advantage of chriftian acquaintance; I
was likewife greatly hindered by a cow-
ardly referved fpirit, I was afraid of being
thought precife, and, though I could not
live without prayer, I durft not propofe
it, even to my wife, till fhe herfelf
firft put me upon it; fo far was I from
thofe expreffions of zeal and love, which
feem fo fuitable to the cafe of one who
has had much forgiven. In a few months
the returning feafon called me abroad
again, and I failed from *L*———, in a
new fhip, *July* 1752.

A fea-faring life is neceffarily excluded
from the benefit of public ordinances and
chriftian communion, but, as I have
obferved, my lofs upon thefe heads was
at this time but fmall. In other refpects,
I know not any calling that feems more
favourable, or affords greater advantages
to an awakened mind, for promoting the
life

life of God in the foul, efpecially to a
perfon who has the command of a fhip,
and thereby has it in his power to reftrain
grofs irregularities in others, and to dif-
pofe of his own time; and ftill more fo
in *African* voyages, as thefe fhips carry a
double proportion of men and officers to
moft others, which made my department
very eafy; and excepting the hurry of
trade, &c. upon the coaft, which is rather
occafional than conftant, afforded me
abundance of leifure. To be at fea in
thefe circumftances, withdrawn out of the
reach of innumerable temptations, with
opportunity and a turn of mind difpofed
to obferve the wonders of God in the
great deep, with the two nobleft objects
of fight, the expanded *heavens*, and the
expanded *ocean* continually in view, and
where evident interpofitions of Divine
Providence, in anfwer to prayer, occur
almoft every day; thefe are helps to
quicken and confirm the life of faith,
which, in a good meafure, fupply to a
religious failor the want of thofe advantages which can be only enjoyed upon
the fhore. And, indeed, though my
knowledge of fpiritual things (as knowledge is ufually eftimated was, at this

time

time, very small, yet I sometimes looked back with regret upon those scenes. I never knew sweeter or more frequent hours of divine communion than in my two last voyages to *Guinea*, when I was either almost secluded from society on shipboard, or when on shore among the natives. I have wandered through the woods, reflecting on the singular goodness of the Lord to me, in a place where, perhaps, there was not a person who knew him for some thousand miles round me. Many a time, upon these occasions, I have restored the beautiful lines of *Propertius* to the right owner, lines full of blasphemy and madness, when addressed to a creature, but full of comfort and propriety in the mouth of a believer.

Sic ego desertis possim bene vivere sylvis
Quo nulla humano sit via trita pede;
Tu mihi curarum requies, in nocte velatra
Lumen, & in solis tu mihi turba locis.

PARAPHRASED.

In desert woods with thee, my God,
Where human footsteps never trod,
   How happy could I be!
Thou my repose from care, my light
Amidst the darkness of the night,
   In solitude my company.

In

In the courfe of this voyage I was wonderfully preferved in the midft of many
obvious and many unforefeen dangers.
At one time there was a confpiracy amongft
my own people to turn pirates, and take
the fhip from me. When the plot was
nearly ripe, and they only waited a convenient opportunity, two of thofe concerned in it were taken ill one day; one
of them died, and he was the only perfon I buried while on board. This fuf-
pended the affair, and opened a way to its
difcovery, or the confequence might have
been fatal. The flaves on board were
likewife frequently plotting infurrections,
and were fometimes upon the very brink
of mifchief; but it was always difclofed in
due time. When I have thought myfelf
moft fecure, I have been fuddenly alarmed
with danger, and when I have almoft de-
fpaired of life, as fudden a deliverance has
been vouchfafed me. My ftay upon the
coaft was long, the trade very precarious,
and, in the purfuit of my bufinefs, both on
board and on fhore, I was *in deaths often.*
Let the following inftance ferve as a fpeci-
men.

I was at a place called *Mana,* near *Cape
Mount,* where I had tranfacted very large
concerns,

concerns, and had, at the time I am
speaking of, some debts and accounts to
settle, which required my attendance on
shore, and I intended to go as the next
morning. When I arose, I left the ship,
according to my purpose; but when I
came near the shore, the surf or beach of
the sea ran so high, that I was almost
afraid to attempt landing. Indeed, I had
often ventured at a worse time, but I felt
an inward hindrance and backwardness,
which I could not account for; the surf
furnished a pretext for indulging it, and
after waiting and hesitating for about half
an hour, I returned to the ship, without
doing any business, which, I think, I never
did but that morning in all the time I
used that trade. But I soon perceived
the reason of all this.—It seems, the day
before I intended to land, a scandalous
and groundless charge had been laid
against me (by whose instigation I could
never learn) which greatly threatened my
honour and interest both in *Africa* and
England, and would, perhaps, humanely
speaking, have affected my life, if I had
landed according to my intention. I shall,
perhaps, inclose a letter, which will give
a full account of this strange adventure,
and

and therefore shall say no more of it here,
any further than to tell you, that an at
tempt, aimed either to destroy my life or
character, and which might very probably in its consequences, have ruined my
voyage, passed off without the least incon-
venience. The person most concerned
owed me about an hundred pounds, which
he sent me in a huff, and otherwise, perhaps would not have paid me at all. I
was very uneasy for a few hours, but
was soon afterwards comforted. I heard
no more of my accusation, till the next
voyage, and then it was publicly acknow-
ledged to have been a malicious calumny,
without the least shadow of a ground.

Such were the vicissitudes and difficulties through which the Lord preserved
me. Now and then both faith and patience were sharply exercised, but suitable
strength was given; and as those things
did not occur every day, the study of the
Latin, of which I gave a general account
in my last, was renewed, and carried on
from time to time, when business would
permit. I was mostly very regular in
the management of my time; I allotted
about eight hours for sleep and meals,
eight hours for exercise and devotion,

G   and

and eight hours to my books, and thus, by diverfifying my engagements, the whole day was agreeably filled up, and I feldom found a day too long, or an hour to fpare. My ftudies kept me employed, and fo far it was. well; otherwife they were hardly worth the time they coft, as they led me to an admiration of falfe models and falfe maxims; an almoft unavoidable confequence, I fuppofe, of an admiration of claffic authors. Abating what I have attained of the language, I think I might have read *Caffandra* or *Cleopatra* to as good purpofe as I read *Livy*, whom I now account an equal *romancer*, though in a different way.

From the coaft I went to St. *Chriftopher's*, and here my idolatrous heart was its own punifhment. The letters I expected from Mrs. ***** were by miftake forwarded to *Antigua*, which had been at firft propofed as our port. As I was certain of her punctuality in writing, if alive, I concluded, by not hearing from her, that fhe was furely dead. This fear affected me more and more, I loft my appetite and reft, I felt an inceffant pain in my ftomach, and in about three weeks time, I was near finking under the weight

of

of an imaginary stroke. I felt some severe symptoms of that mixture of pride and madness, which is commonly called *a broken heart*; and indeed I wonder that this case is not more common than it appears to be. How often do the potsherds of the earth presume to contend with their Maker? And what a wonder of mercy is it that they are not all broken? However, my complaint was not all grief, conscience had a share. I thought my unfaithfulness to God had deprived me of her, especially my backwardness in speaking of spiritual things, which I could hardly attempt even to her. It was this thought, that I had lost invalu. e irrecoverable opportunities, which both duty and affection should have engaged me to improve that chiefly stung me, and I thought I would have given the world to know she was living, that I might at least discharge my engagements by writing, though I were never to see her again. This was a sharp lesson, but I hope it did me good; and when I had thus suffered some weeks, I thought of sending a small vessel to *Antigua*. I did so, and she brought me several packets, which restored my health and peace, and gave me a strong

contrast

contraſt of the Lord's goodneſs to me, and my unbelief and ingratitude towards him.

In *Auguſt* 1753, I returned to *L——.* My ſtay was very ſhort at home, that voyage only ſix weeks; in that ſpace nothing very memorable occurred; I ſhall therefore begin my next with an account of my third and laſt voyage. And thus I give both you and myſelf hopes of a ſpeedy period to theſe memoirs, which begin to be tedious and minute, even to myſelf, only I am animated by the thought that I write at your requeſt, and have therefore an opportunity of ſhewing my-ſelf,

Your obliged ſervant,

JANUARY 31, 1763.

LETTER

LETTER XIII.

DEAR SIR,

MY third voyage was shorter and less perplexed than either of the former. Before I sailed, I met with a young man who had formerly been a midshipman, and my intimate companion on board the *Harwich*. He was, at the time I first knew him, a sober youth, but I found too much success in my unhappy attempts to infect him with libertine principles. When we met at *L*———, our acquaintance renewed upon the ground of our former intimacy. He had good sense, and had read many books. Our conversation frequently turned upon religion, and I was very desirous to repair the mischief I had done him. I gave him a plain account of the manner and reason of my change, and used every argument to persuade him to relinquish his infidel schemes: and when I sometimes pressed him so close that he had no other reply

G 3

to make, he would remind me that I was the very firft perfon who had given him an idea of his liberty. This occafioned me many mournful reflections. He was then going mafter to *Guinea* himfelf, but before his fhip was ready, his merchant became a bankrupt, which difconcerted his voyage. As he had no further expectations for that year, I offered to take him with me as a companion, that he might gain a knowledge of the coaft; and the gentleman who employed me promifed to provide for him upon his return. My view in this was not fo much to ferve him in his bufinefs, as to have an opportunity of debating the point with him at leifure; and I hoped in the courfe of my voyage, my arguments, example, and prayers, might have fome good effect on him. My intention in this ftep was better than my judgment, and I had frequent reafon to repent it. He was exceedingly profane, and grew worfe and worfe; I faw in him a moft lively picture of what I had once been, but it was very inconvenient to have it always before my eyes. Befides, he was not only deaf to my remonftrances himfelf, but laboured all he could to counteract my influence upon
others.

others. His spirit and passions were likewise exceeding high, so that it required
all my prudence and authority to hold
him in any degree of restraint. He was
as a sharp thorn in my side for some
time; but at length I had opportunity
upon the coast, of buying a small vessel,
which I supplied with a cargo from my
own, and gave him the command, and
sent him away to trade on the ship's account. When we parted, I repeated and
enforced my best advice. I believe his
friendship and regard was as great as could
be expected, where principles were so dia-
metrically opposite; he seemed greatly
affected when I left him, but my words
had no weight with him; when he found
himself at liberty from under my eye,
he gave a hasty loose to every appetite;
and his violent irregularities, joined to
the heat of the climate, soon threw him
into a malignant fever, which carried him
off in a few days. He died convinced,
but not changed. The account I had
from those who were with him was dreadful; his rage and despair struck them all
with horror, and he pronounced his own
fatal doom before he expired, without
any appearance that he either *hoped* or

asked

asked for mercy. I thought this awful contrast might not be improper to give you, as a stronger view of the distinguishing goodness of God to me, the chief of sinners.

I left the coast in about four months, and sailed for St. *Christopher*'s. Hitherto I had enjoyed a perfect state of health, equally in every climate, for several years: but, upon this passage, I was visited with a fever, which gave me a very near prospect of eternity: I have obtained liberty to inclose you three or four letters, which will more clearly illustrate the state and measure of my experience, at different times, than any thing I can say at present. One of them you will find was wrote at this period, when I could hardly hold a pen, and had some reason to believe I should write no more. I had not that πληροφρια*, which is so desirable at a time when flesh and heart fail; but my hopes were greater than my fears, and I felt a silent composure of spirit, which enabled me to wait the event without much anxiety. My trust, though weak in degree, was alone fixed upon

* Full assurance.

the blood and righteousnefs of Jefus, and thofe words, " he is able to fave to the uttermoft," gave me great relief. I was for a while troubled with `a very fingular thought—whether it was a temptation, or that the fever difordered my faculties, I cannot fay, but I feemed not fo much afraid of wrath and punifhment, as of being loft and overlooked amidft the myriads that are continually entering the unfeen world. What is my foul, thought I, amongft fuch an innumerable multitude of beings! And this troubled me greatly. Perhaps the Lord will take no notice of me. I was perplexed thus for fome time, but at laft a text of fcripture, very appofite to the cafe, occurred to my mind, and put an end to the doubt: " The Lord knoweth them that are his." In about ten days, beyond the hopes of thofe about me, I began to amend, and by the time of our arrival in the *Weft Indies* I was perfectly recovered.—I hope this vifitation was made ufeful to me.

Thus far, that is, for about the fpace of fix years, the Lord was pleafed to lead me in a fecret way.—I had learnt fomething of the evil of my heart: I

had

had read the Bible over and over, with
several good books, and had a general
view of the *gospel truth*. But my conceptions were, in many respects, confused;
not having, in all this time, met with one
acquaintance who could assist my inqui-
ries. But upon my arrival at St. *Christopher's*, this voyage, I found a Captain of
a ship from *London*, whose conversation
was greatly helpful to me. He was, and
is a member of Mr. *B———r's* church, a
man of experience in the things of God
and of a lively communicative turn. We
discovered each other by some casual expressions in mixed company, and soon
became (so far as business would permit)
inseparable. For near a month we spent
every evening together on board each
other's ship alternately, and often pro-
longed our visits till towards day-break.
I was all *ears*; and what was better, he
not only informed my understanding, but
his discourse inflamed my heart.—He
encouraged me to open my mouth in
social prayer, he taught me the advantage of christian converse; he put me
upon an attempt to make my profession
more public, and to venture to speak
for God. From him, or rather from
the

the Lord, by his means, I received an increafe of knowledge; my conceptions became clearer and more evangelical, and I was delivered from a fear which had long troubled me, the fear of relapfing into my former apoftafy. But now I began to underftand the fecurity of the covenant of grace, and to expect to be preferved, not by my own power and holinefs, but by the mighty power and promife of God, through faith in an unchangeable Saviour. He likewife gave me a general view of the ftate of religion, with the errors and controverfies of the times (things to which I had been entirely a ftranger) and finally, directed me where to inquire in *London* for further inftruction, with thefe new acquired advantages, I left him, and my paffage homewards gave me leifure to digeft what I had received; I had much comfort and freedom during thofe feven weeks, and my fun was feldom clouded. I arrived fafe in *L———*, *Auguft* 1754.

My ftay at home was intended to be but fhort, and by the beginning of *November*, I was ready again for the fea; but the Lord faw fit to over-rule my defign. During the time I was engaged

G 6

in the flave trade, I never had the leaft
fcruple as to its lawfulnefs; I was, upon
the whole, fatisfied with it, as the ap-
pointment Providence had marked out
for me; yet it was, in many refpects, far
from eligible. It is, indeed, accounted
a genteel employment, and is ufually
very profitable, though to me it did not
prove fo, the Lord feeing that a large
increafe of wealth could not be good for
me. However, I confidered myfelf as
a fort of *Gaoler* or *Turnkey*: and I was
fometimes fhocked with an employment
that was perpetually converfant with
chains, bolts and fhackles. In this view
I had often petitioned, in my prayers,
that the Lord (in his own time) would be
pleafed to fix me in a more humane calling,
and (if it might be) place me where I
might have more frequent converfe with
his people and ordinances, and be freed
from thofe-long feparations from home,
which very often were hard to bear: my
prayers were now anfwered, though in a
way I little expected. I now experienced
another fudden unforefeen change of life:
I was within two days of failing, and, to
all appearance in good health as ufual;
but, in the afternoon as I was fitting

with

with Mrs. ******, by ourfelves drinking tea, and talking over paft events, I was in a moment feized with a fit, which deprived me of fenfe and motion, and left me no other fign of life than that of breathing—— I fuppofe it was of the apoplectic kind.—— It lafted about an hour, and when I recovered, it left a pain and dizzinefs in my head, which continued with fuch fymptoms, as induced the phyficians to judge it would not be fafe or prudent for me to proceed on the voyage. Accordingly, by the advice of my friend, to whom the fhip belonged, I refigned the command the day before fhe failed, and thus I was unexpectedly called from that fervice, and freed from a fhare of the future confequences of that voyage; which proved extremely calamitous. The perfon who went in my room, moft of the officers, and many of the crew died, and the veffel was brought home with great difficulty.

As I was now difengaged from bufinefs, I left L————, and fpent moft of the following year at *London*, and in *Kent*. But I entered upon a new trial.——You will eafily conceive that Mrs. ****** was not an unconcerned fpectator, when I lay extended, and, as fhe thought, expiring

upon

upon the ground. In effect, the blow
that ftruck me reached her in the fame
inftant, fhe did not indeed, immediately
feel it till her apprehenfions on my account began to fubfide; but as I grew better, fhe became worfe: her furprize threw
her into a diforder, which no phyficians
could define, or medicines remove. Without any of the ordinary fymptoms of a
confumption, fhe decayed almoft vifibly
till fhe became fo weak that fhe could
hardly bear any one to walk acrofs the
room fhe was in. I was placed for about
eleven months in what Dr. *Young* calls the

> "—dreadful poft of obfervation,
> " Darker every hour."

It was not till after my fettlement in
my prefent ftation that the Lord was
pleafed to reftore her by his own hand,
when all hopes from ordinary means
were at an end. But before this took
place, I have fome other particulars to
mention, which muft be the fubject of
the following fheet, which I hope will be
the laft on this fubject from

Your affectionate fervant.

February 1, 1763.

LETTER

LETTER XIV.

DEAR SIR,

BY the directions I had received from my friend at St. *Kitt's*, I soon found out a religious acquaintance in *London*. I first applied to Mr. *B———*, and chiefly attended upon his ministry, when in town. From him I received many helps both in public and private; for he was pleased to favour me with his friendship from the first His kindness and the intimacy between us has continued and increased to this day, and of all my many friends, I am most deeply indebted to him. The late Mr. *H———d* was my second acquaintance; a man of a choice spirit, and an abundant zeal for the Lord's service. I enjoyed his correspondence till near the time of his death. Soon after, upon Mr. *W———d's* return from *America*, my two good friends introduced me to him; and though I had little personal acquaintance with him till afterwards, his ministry was exceedingly useful to me. I had likewise

wife accefs to fome religious focieties, and
became known to many excellent chriftians in private life. Thus when at
London, I lived at the fountain-head, as
it were, for fpiritual advantages. When
I was in *Kent* it was very different, yet I
found fome ferious perfons there ; but
the fine variegated woodland country
afforded me advantages of another kind.
Moft of my time, at leaft fome houis
every day, I paffed in retirement, when
the weather was fair, fometimes in the
thickeft woods, fometimes on the higheft
hills, where almoft every ftep varied the
profpect. It has been my cuftom, for
many years, to perform my devotional-
exercifes *fub dio*, when I have opportunity,
and I always find thefe rural fcenes have
fome tendency, both to refrefh and compofe my fpirits. A beautiful diverfified
profpect gladdens my heait. When I
am withdiawn from the noife and petty
works of men, I confider myfelf as in the
great temple, which the Lord has built for
his own honour.

The country between *Rochefter* and
Maidftone, bordering upon the *Medway*,
was well fuited to the turn of my mind;
and was I to go over it now, I could

point

point to many a place where I remember
to have either earneftly fought, or happily
found, the Lord's comfortable prefence
with my foul. And thus I lived, fometimes at *London*, and fometimes in the
country, till the autumn of the following year. All this while I had two
trials, more or lefs, upon my mind; the
firft and principal was Mrs. ******'s
illnefs; fhe ftill grew worfe, and I had
daily more reafon to fear, that the hour
of feparation was at hand. When faith
was in exercife, I was in fome meafure
refigned to the Lord's will; but too
often my heart rebelled, and I found it
hard, either to truft or to fubmit. I had
likewife fome care about my future fettlement; the *African* trade was overdone
that year, and my friends did not care to
fit out another fhip till mine returned.
I was fome time in fufpenfe, but, indeed,
a provifion of food and raiment has feldom been a caufe of great folicitude to
me. I found it eafier to truft the Lord
in this point than in the former, and accordingly this was firft anfwered. In
Auguft I received an account, that I was
nominated to the office of —————.
Thefe places are ufually obtained, or at

leaſt ſought, by dint of much intereſt and application, but this came to me unſought and unexpected. I knew, indeed, my good friend in L——— had endeavoured to procure another poſt for me, but found it pre engaged. I found afterwards, that the place I had miſſed would have been very unſuitable for me, and that this, which I had no thought of, was the very thing I could have wiſhed for, affording me much leiſure, and the liberty of living in my own way. Several circumſtances, unnoticed by others, concurred to ſhew me, that the good hand of the Lord was as remarkably concerned in this event as in any other leading turn of my life.

But when I gained this point, my diſtreſs in the other was doubled; I was obliged to leave Mrs. ******, in the greateſt extremity of pain and illneſs, when the phyſicians could do no more, and I had no ground of hope, that I ſhould ſee her again alive, but this—that nothing is impoſſible with the Lord. I had a ſevere conflict, but faith prevailed: I found the promiſe remarkably fulfilled, of ſtrength proportioned to my need. The day before I ſet out, and not till then,

then, the burden was entirely taken from
my mind; I was ftrengthened to refign
both her and myfelf to the Lord's difpo-
fal, and departed fiom her in a cheerful
frame. Soon after I was gone fhe began
to amend, and recoveied fo faft, that in
about two months I had the pleafure
to meet her at *Stone,* on her journey to
L————.

And now I think I have anfwered, if
not exceeded your defire. Since- *October*
1755, we have been comfortably fettled
here, and all my circumftances have been
as remarkably fmooth and uniform as
they were various in former years. My
trials have been light and few — not but
that I ftill find in the experience of every
day the neceffity of a life of faith. My
principal trial is — the body of fin and
death, which makes me often to figh out
the apoftle's complaint, " O wretched
man !" But with him likewife I can
fay, " I thank God through Jefus Chrift
my Lord." I live in a barren land,
where the knowledge and power of the
gofpel is very low, yet here are a few of
the Lord's people, and this wildernefs
has been a ufeful fchool to me, where I
have ftudied more leifurely the truths I

gathered

gathered up in *London*. I brought down
with me a confiderable ftock of notional
truth, but I have fince found, that there
is no effectual teacher but God, that we
can receive no farther than he is pleafed
to communicate; and that no knowledge
is truly ufeful to me, but what is made
my own by experience. Many things,
I thought I had learned, would not ftand
in an hour of temptation, till I had in this
way learned them over again. Since the
year 1757, I have had an increafing acquaintance in the Weft Riding of *York-
fhire*, where the gofpel flourifhes greatly.
This has been a good fchool to me: I
have converfed at large among all parties without joining any; and in my attempts to hit the *golden mean*, I have
fometimes been drawn too near the different extremes; yet the Lord has enabled me to profit by my miftakes. In
brief, I am ftill a learner, and the Lord
ftill condefcends to teach me. I begin
at length to fee that I have attained but
very little, but I truft in him to carry on
his own work in my foul, and by all the
difpenfations of his grace and providence
to increafe my knowledge of him and of
myfelf.

When

When I was fixed in a houfe, and found
my bufinefs would afford me much leifure time, I confidered in what manner I
fhould improve it. And now having
reafon to clofe with the apoftle's determination, " to know nothing but Jefus
Chrift and him crucified," I devoted
my life to the profecution of fpiritual
knowledge, and refolved to purfue nothing but in fubfervience to this main defign. This refolution divorced me (as I
have already hinted) from the claffics and
mathematics. My firft attempt was to
learn fo much *Greek*, as would enable
me to underftand the *New Teftament* and
Septuagint; and when I had made fome
progrefs this way, I entered upon the *Hebrew* the following year; and two years
afterwards having furmifed fome advantages from the *Syriac* verfion, I began
with that language. You muft not think
that I have attained, or ever aimed at a
critical fkill in any of thefe; I had no bufinefs with them, but as in reference to
fomething elfe. I never read one claffic
author in the *Greek*; I thought it too late
in life to take fuch a round in this language, as I had done in the *Latin*. I only
wanted the fignification of fcriptural words
and

and phrafes, and for this I thought I might avail myfelf of *Scapula*, the *Synopfis*, and others, who had fuftained the drudgery before me. In the *Hebrew* I can read the hiftorical books and pfalms, with tolerable eafe, but in the prophetical and difficult parts, I am frequently obliged to have recourfe to *Lexicons*, &c. However I know fo much as to be able, with fuch helps as are at hand, to judge for myfelf the meaning of any paffage I have occafion to confult. Beyond this I do not think of proceeding, if I can find better employment; for I would rather be fome way ufeful to others, than die with the reputation of an eminent linguift.

Together with thefe ftudies, I have kept up a courfe of reading of the beft writers in divinity that have come to my hand, in the *Latin* and *Englifh* tongue, and fome *French* (for I picked up the *French* at times, while I ufed the fea). But within thefe two or three years I have accuftomed myfelf chiefly to writing, and have not found time to read many books befides the fcripture.

I am the more particular in this account, as my cafe has been fomething fingular; for in all my literary attempts I have been obliged to ftrike out my own path, by the light I could acquire from books, as I have

not

not had a teacher or affistant fince I was ten years of age.

One word concerning my views to the *miniftry*, and I have done. I have told you, that this was my dear mother's hope concerning me; but her death, and the fcenes of life in which I afterwards engaged, feemed to cut off the probability. The firft defires of this fort in my own mind, arofe many years ago, from a reflection on *Gal.* i. 23, 24. I could but wifh for fuch a public opportunity to teftify the riches of divine grace. I thought I was, above moft living, a fit perfon to proclaim that faithful faying, " That Jefus Chrift came into the world to fave the chief of finners;" and as my life had been full of remarkable turns, and I feemed felected to fhew what the Lord could do, I was in fome hopes that, perhaps, fooner or later, he might call me into his fervice.

I believe it was a diftant hope of this, that determined me to ftudy the original fcriptures; but it remained an imperfect defire in my own breaft, till it was recommended to me by fome chriftian friends. I ftarted at the thought, when firft ferioufly propofed to me; but afterwards fet apart fome weeks to confider the cafe, to confult my friends, and to intreat
the

the Lord's direction.—The judgment of my friends, and many things that occurred, tended to engage me. My firſt thought was to join the diſſenters, from a preſumption that I could not honeſtly make the required ſubſcriptions; but Mr. C——, in a converſation upon theſe points, moderated my ſcruples; and preferring the eſtabliſhed church in ſome other reſpects, I accepted a title from him, ſome months afterwards, and ſolicited ordination from the late Archbiſhop of *York*: I need not tell you I met a refuſal, nor what ſteps I took afterwards, to ſucceed elſewhere. At preſent I deſiſt from any applications. My deſire to ſerve the Lord is not weakened; but I am not ſo haſty to puſh myſelf forward as I was formerly. It is ſufficient that he knows how to diſpoſe of me, and that he both can and will do what is beſt. To him I commend myſelf: I truſt that his will and my true intereſt are inſeparable. To his name be glory for ever. And thus I conclude my ſtory, and preſume you will acknowledge I have been particular enough. I have room for no more, but to repeat that

I am, Sir, Your's, &c.

FEBRUARY 2, 1763.

THE END

CPSIA information can be obtained at www.ICGtesting.com
Printed in the USA
LVOW02s2128251213

366807LV00006B/276/P

9 781140 775386